educamos·sm

Caro aluno, seja bem-vindo à sua plataforma do conhecimento!

A partir de agora, você tem à sua disposição uma plataforma que reúne, em um só lugar, recursos educacionais digitais que complementam os livros impressos e são desenvolvidos especialmente para auxiliar você em seus estudos. Veja como é fácil e rápido acessar os recursos deste projeto.

1 Faça a ativação dos códigos dos seus livros.

Se você NÃO tiver cadastro na plataforma:

- Para acessar os recursos digitais, você precisa estar cadastrado na plataforma educamos.sm. Em seu computador, acesse o endereço <**br.educamos.sm**>.
- No canto superior direito, clique em "**Primeiro acesso? Clique aqui**". Para iniciar o cadastro, insira o código indicado abaixo.
- Depois de incluir todos os códigos, clique em "**Registrar-se**" e, em seguida, preencha o formulário para concluir esta etapa.

Se você JÁ fez cadastro na plataforma:

- Em seu computador, acesse a plataforma e faça o *login* no canto superior direito.
- Em seguida, você visualizará os livros que já estão ativados em seu perfil. Clique no botão "**Adicionar livro**" e insira o código abaixo.

CB123852

Este é o seu código de ativação! →

D7XZT-EAZBR-AAABP

2 Acesse os recursos.

Usando um computador

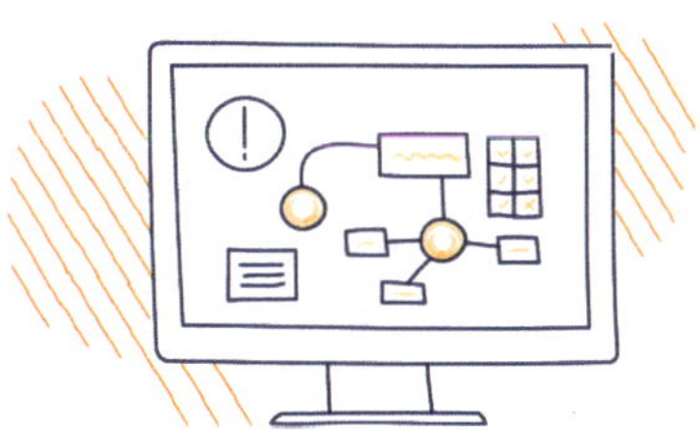

Acesse o endereço <**br.educamos.sm**> e faça o *login* no canto superior direito. Nessa página, você visualizará todos os seus livros cadastrados. Para acessar o livro desejado, basta clicar na sua capa.

Usando um dispositivo móvel

Instale o aplicativo **educamos.sm**, que está disponível gratuitamente na loja de aplicativos do dispositivo. Utilize o mesmo *login* e a mesma senha da plataforma para acessar o aplicativo.

Importante! Não se esqueça de sempre cadastrar seus livros da SM em seu perfil. Assim, você garante a visualização dos seus conteúdos, seja no computador, seja no dispositivo móvel. Em caso de dúvida, entre em contato com nosso canal de atendimento pelo **telefone 0800 72 54876** ou pelo ***e-mail* atendimento@grupo-sm.com**.

219727_15

sm

It Fits Inglês 8º Ano. - Ensino Fundamental: Anos Finais - Livro Digital do Aluno - 4ª Edição 2024

IT FITS

8

**COMPONENTE CURRICULAR:
LÍNGUA INGLESA**

**ENSINO FUNDAMENTAL
ANOS FINAIS
8º ANO**

Editora responsável: Ana Luiza Couto

- Licenciada em Letras - Língua e Literatura Portuguesa pela Universidade Federal do Pará (UFPA).
- Pós-graduada em Tradução Inglês-Português pelo Centro Universitário Ibero-Americano (SP).
- Editora de livros didáticos.

Organizadora: SM Educação

Obra coletiva concebida, desenvolvida e produzida por SM Educação.

São Paulo, 4ª edição, 2022

"Em respeito ao meio ambiente, as folhas deste livro foram produzidas com fibras obtidas de árvores de florestas plantadas, com origem certificada"

Direção editorial Cláudia Carvalho Neves
Gerência editorial Lia Monguilhott Bezerra
Gerência de *design* e produção André Monteiro
Edição executiva Ana Luiza Couto
Edição: Barbara Manholeti, Gabriela Damico Zarantonello
Assistência de edição: Natália Feulo
Suporte editorial: Fernanda de Araújo Fortunato
Coordenação de preparação e revisão Cláudia Rodrigues do Espírito Santo
Preparação: Andréa Vidal
Revisão: Andréa Vidal, Patricia Cordeiro e Luciana Chagas
Coordenação de *design* Gilciane Munhoz
***Design*:** Tiago Stéfano, João Brito e Paula Maestro
Coordenação de arte Andressa Fiorio
Edição de arte: Bruno Cesar Guimarães e Fernando Fernandes
Assistência de produção: Júlia Stacciarini Teixeira
Coordenação de iconografia Josiane Laurentino
Pesquisa iconográfica: Camila D'Angelo e Junior Rozzo
Tratamento de imagem: Marcelo Casaro
Capa Thatiana Kalaes
Ilustração da capa: Carlos Lehmann
Projeto gráfico Gilciane Munhoz
Pré-impressão Américo Jesus
Fabricação Alexander Maeda
Impressão Bartira

Elaboração de originais

Ana Luiza Couto
Licenciada em Letras – Língua e Literatura Portuguesa pela Universidade Federal do Pará (UFPA).
Pós-graduada em Tradução Inglês-Português pelo Centro Universitário Ibero-Americano (SP).
Editora de materiais didáticos.

Barbara Cristina Manholeti
Bacharela em Letras – Línguas Portuguesa e Russa pela Faculdade de Filosofia, Letras e Ciências Humanas (FFLCH) da Universidade de São Paulo (USP).
Editora de materiais didáticos.

Em respeito ao meio ambiente, as folhas deste livro foram produzidas com fibras obtidas de árvores de florestas plantadas, com origem certificada.

Dados Internacionais de Catalogação na Publicação (CIP)
(Câmara Brasileira do Livro, SP, Brasil)

It Fits : 8º ano : ensino fundamental : anos finais / editora responsável Ana Luiza Couto ; organizadora SM Educação ; obra coletiva concebida, desenvolvida e produzida por SM Educação. — 4. ed. — São Paulo : Edições SM, 2022.

Componente curricular: Língua inglesa.
ISBN 978-65-5744-711-6 (aluno)
ISBN 978-65-5744-712-3 (professor)

1. Inglês (Ensino fundamental) I. Couto, Ana Luiza.

22-112016 CDD-372.652

Índices para catálogo sistemático:
1. Inglês : Ensino fundamental 372.652

Cibele Maria Dias - Bibliotecária - CRB-8/9427

4ª edição, 2022
1ª impressão, setembro 2023

SM Educação
Avenida Paulista, 1842 – 18º andar, cj. 185, 186 e 187 – Condomínio Cetenco Plaza
Bela Vista 01310-945 São Paulo SP Brasil
Tel. 11 2111-7400
atendimento@grupo-sm.com
www.grupo-sm.com/br

Apresentação

Olá,

Bem-vindo a esta coleção! Assim como você, nós também já estudamos inglês, e não poderíamos deixar essa experiência de lado. Como seria o livro que gostaríamos de ter tido? Que temas gostaríamos de ter discutido nas aulas? Sobre o que gostaríamos de ter lido? Ao idealizar esta coleção, procuramos incluir alguns dos itens que gostaríamos de ter visto nos materiais didáticos com os quais tivemos contato, sempre com a preocupação de abordar tudo isso de acordo com o contexto atual.

Algo que tivemos muito claro durante a produção desta coleção é a crença de que sua aprendizagem não poderia ficar restrita à língua. Queríamos levar até você um pouco do que acontece por aí, criar oportunidades de troca de experiências e aguçar sua curiosidade, para tornar sua experiência escolar interessante dentro e fora da sala de aula.

Talvez você não saiba, mas 80% dos falantes de inglês não têm esse idioma como língua materna. Não é curioso? É por isso que o inglês é chamado de “língua franca” e é usado como meio de comunicação por povos de muitas nações e culturas diferentes. Pessoas de várias partes do mundo usam inglês no trabalho, na escola, em suas viagens, ao conversar com pessoas de outros países pela Internet, pelo telefone...

Explore bastante esta coleção nas aulas e, especialmente, fora delas. Como fazer isso? Ouvindo os áudios, relendo os textos, consultando o glossário e visitando os *sites* de onde muitos textos foram extraídos.

Por último, algo muito importante: para deixar a coleção interativa, criamos um tutor, um simpático robozinho que “conversa” com você em vários momentos do livro. Ele chega a você sem um nome; portanto, sua primeira missão é escolher uma identidade para ele. *Be creative*!

Enjoy the book!

Vamos conhecer a coleção?

A unidade sempre inicia com um desafio. Você vai folhear as páginas e fazer uma busca de imagens. É um *quick challenge* de aquecimento, de preparação.

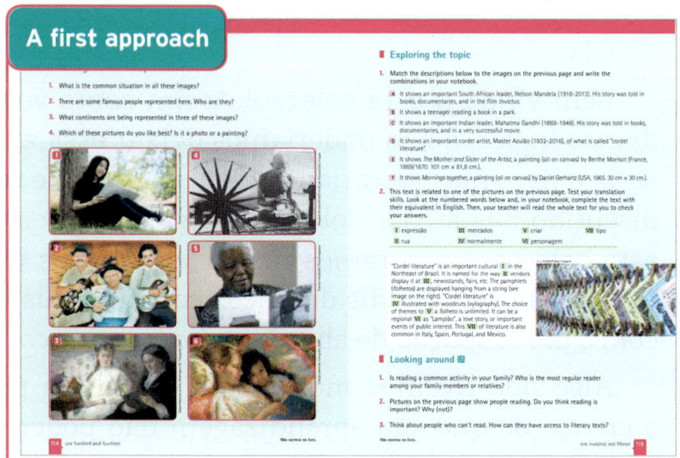

A first approach

Esta é uma primeira abordagem mais detalhada do tema da unidade. Você começa a aprender muitas coisas com base na observação de um conjunto de imagens e usa muito o conhecimento que você já tem sobre o tema.

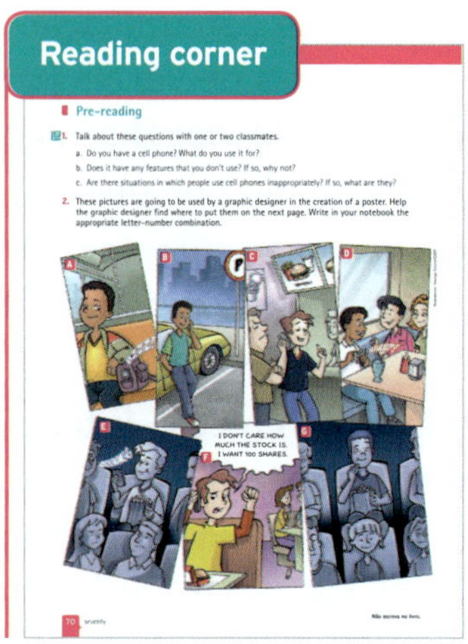

Reading corner

Uma parte importantíssima no aprendizado de línguas é a leitura. Nesta seção, você tem oportunidade de desenvolver habilidades que o ajudarão a compreender vários tipos de texto em inglês.

Words, words, words

Nesta seção, apresentamos vários tipos de palavras ligadas ao tema da unidade. Aquilo que você já sabe é sempre aproveitado como um meio de ampliar seu repertório.

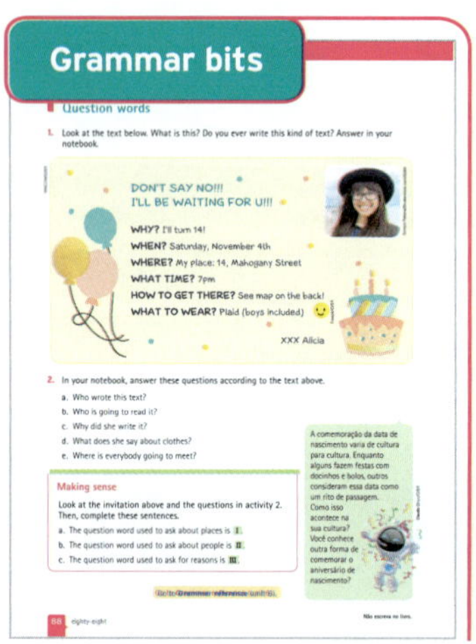

Grammar bits

Nesta seção, você é desafiado a "descobrir" como funciona a gramática nos textos apresentados na unidade. Você levanta hipóteses e usa a lógica e seu conhecimento prévio para aprender a gramática.

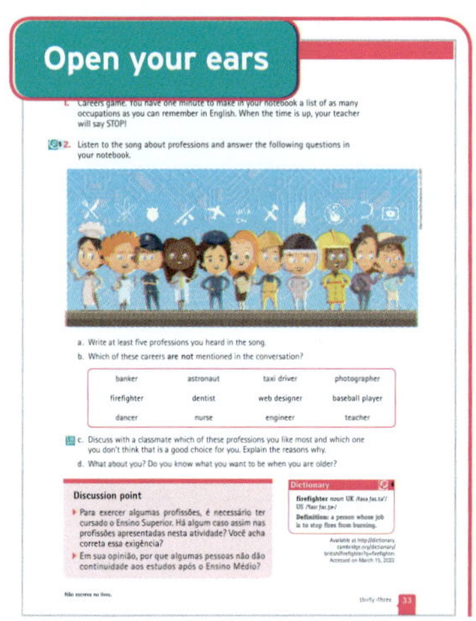

Open your ears

Prepare seus ouvidos: é momento de ouvir. Você estará envolvido em atividades interessantes e variadas de compreensão oral. São diálogos, monólogos, propagandas, poemas, músicas...

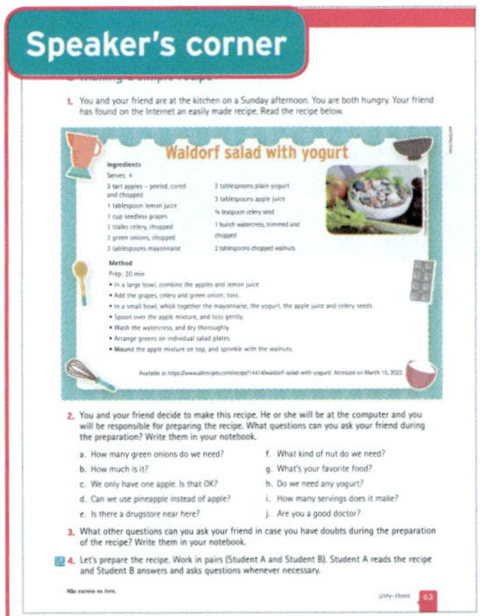

Speaker's corner

Há oportunidades de falar inglês em todas as seções do livro, mas é nesta seção que essa importante habilidade é abordada com mais objetividade. Você é convidado a interagir oralmente em inglês com os colegas nas mais variadas situações.

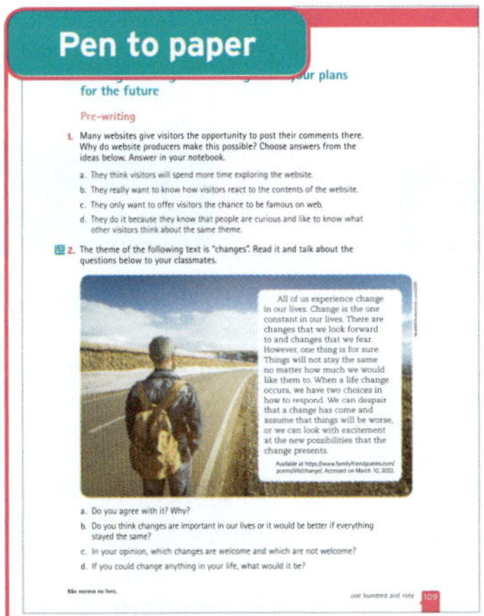

Pen to paper

A habilidade da escrita é abordada nesta seção. Você vai produzir textos de diferentes gêneros, seguindo passos importantes que garantirão um bom resultado. Esses passos orientam você nas diversas fases da escrita.

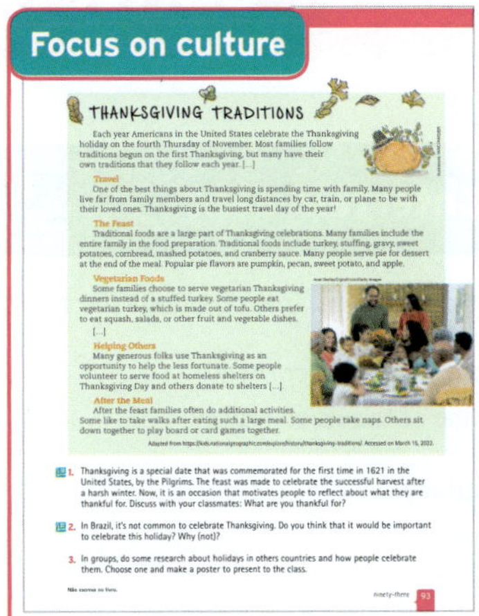

Focus on culture

Nesta seção, você vai ter contato com a dimensão intercultural da língua inglesa e sua presença no mundo. Para que pessoas de países diversos se entendam, não basta falar o mesmo idioma. Conhecer as diferenças culturais aproxima os povos, evita mal-entendidos e facilita a comunicação.

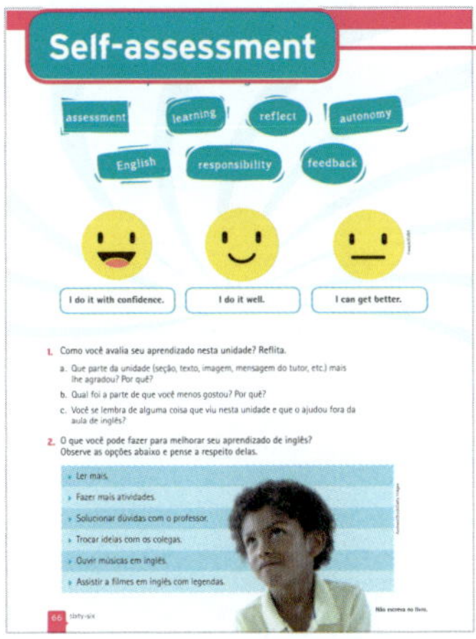

Self-assessment

Trata-se de uma autoavaliação, um momento em que você é convidado a parar um pouco, voltar à unidade e refletir sobre os procedimentos de estudo e seu desempenho nas atividades realizadas. Você se avalia e assim vai se tornando mais independente.

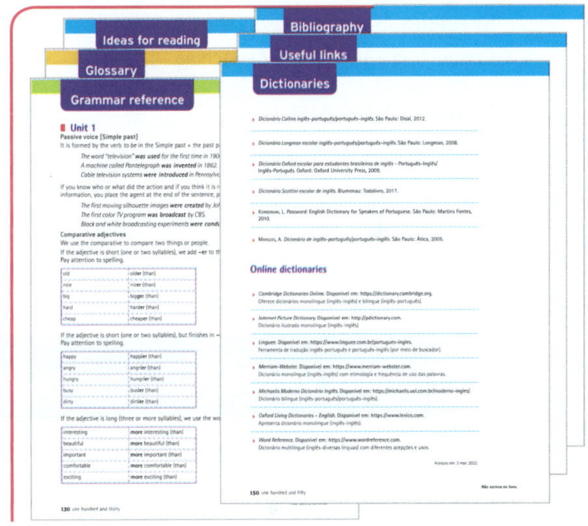

Ao final do livro, você encontra as seções **Grammar reference**, **Glossary**, **Ideas for reading**, **Dictionaries**, **Useful links** e **Bibliography**, que podem ser consultadas sempre que você tiver alguma dúvida ou quiser enriquecer seu aprendizado.

Toda unidade traz sempre um verbete, com apresentação de dicionário bilíngue. Você vê a transcrição fonética e vê a tradução para o português. Compreender os símbolos fonéticos faz parte do desenvolvimento da competência linguística. Você também pode ouvir a pronúncia dessas palavras nos áudios.

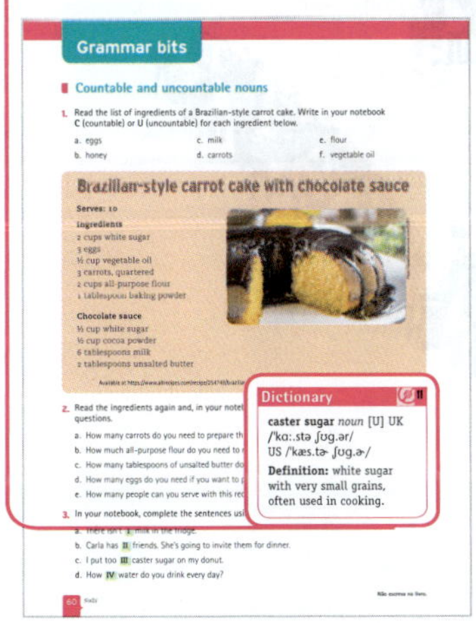

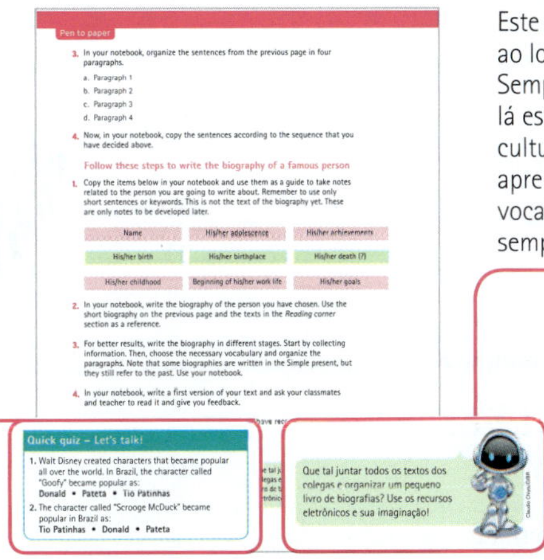

A proposta da coleção é ensinar inglês de maneira descontraída. Há jogos, textos divertidos, desafios... O *Quick quiz – Let's talk!* é um desafio rápido que aparece em todas as unidades para testar seus conhecimentos culturais, científicos e linguísticos, entre outros.

Ícones

Atividade oral

2 Áudio

Este sou eu, seu companheiro ao longo de toda a coleção. Sempre que for oportuno, lá estarei, dando dicas culturais, de estratégias de aprendizagem, pronúncia, vocabulário... Sou um tutor sempre pronto a ajudá-lo.

Claudio Chiyo/ID/BR

Table of contents

Hobbit/Shutterstock.com/ID/BR

Não escreva no livro.

Claudio Chiyo/ID/BR

Suryara Bernardi/ID/BR

YANCOM/ID/BR

Claudio Chiyo/ID/BR

Não escreva no livro.

UNIT

1 Entertainment

In this unit you will have contact with different texts and activities related to television and cinema. The main text is about the history of one of the most popular means of communication in the world: the television. All over the unit you will be engaged in activities that feature the following elements:

- **Genres:** timeline; film review; survey
- **Vocabulary:** TV programs; film genres
- **Grammar:** passive voice; comparative adjectives

Quick challenge

Read the questions below. Then, scan the pages of unit 1 and answer the following questions in your notebook.

a. What is the title of the text in the *Reading corner* section?

b. Which page is the photo of the TV series *Everybody hates Chris* on?

c. Which section(s) are there images of movie posters in?

d. One of these pictures is not used in this unit. Which one?

1

NIkada/iStock/Getty Images

2

Zaptik/Shutterstock.com/ID/BR

3

Claudio Chyio/ID/BR

Não escreva no livro.

A first approach

Talking about the topic

1. Which of these ways of entertainment do you like the most? Why?
2. What are the positive aspects of some of these ways of entertainment?
3. In which of these situations can people learn or practice English?
4. Look at these images for one minute. Cover them with a sheet of paper or close your book. Then use your memory to describe as many pictures as you can.

1

MBI/Shutterstock.com/ID/BR

2

Nelen/Shutterstock.com/ID/BR

3

Artistan/iStock/Getty Images

4

Sergey Novikov/Shutterstock.com/ID/BR

5

Deklofenak/iStock/Getty Images

6

Nikada/iStock/Getty Images

Não escreva no livro.

Exploring the topic

1. Look at these activities and decide which one corresponds to each group of words below. Write the answer in your notebook.

reading | going out with friends | watching TV | surfing the Internet | listening to music

a. band / song / earphone
b. cartoon / quiz show / video clip
c. magazine / novel / newspaper
d. chat room / online game / Instant Messenger
e. eating out / park / cinema

2. Which of the five activities above is your favorite? Share it with a classmate.

3. Read each statement below. In your notebook, write **I agree**, **I don't agree** or **I don't know**. Then, explain your answers to a classmate.

a. People spend too much time in front of screens.
b. It is more interesting to read an e-book than to read a paper book.
c. It is very important that our parents choose what we watch on TV.

Looking around

1. Which TV show produced in Brazil do you like the most? Do you think your classmates like it as well? How about your teacher?

2. Use your imagination. What do you think these people are watching on TV? How do you know?

MBI/Shutterstock.com/ID/BR

Dragon Images/Shutterstock.com/ID/BR

Image Source/Getty Images

Não escreva no livro.

Reading corner

Pre-reading

1. These pictures show some facts about the history of television. In what order do you think these events happened?

A

HSNphotography/Shutterstock.com/ID/BR

DVDs become popular.

C

Bridgeman Images/Fotoarena

Black and white TV set.

E

Think4photop/Shutterstock.com/ID/BR

Smart TV set.

B

4X5 Coll-PR Productions 1991/Superstock/Imageplus

VCR becomes popular.

D

CMCD/ID/ES

Remote control is invented.

F

Maximilian Stock Ltd./SPL/Fotoarena

First color TV program.

Exploring the text

1. Read this timeline and find the lines that correspond to the six pictures above. Then, write in your notebook the combination of year and letter.

Dictionary 1

broadcasting *noun* UK /ˈbrɔːdkaːstiŋ/

Definition: the transmission of programmes or information by radio or television.

Available at https://en.oxforddictionaries.com/definition/broadcasting. Accessed on March 10, 2022.

A timeline of television history

- **1900** The word *television* was used for the first time in Paris.
- **1930s** Black and white broadcasting experiments were conducted by RCA.
- **1948** Cable television systems were introduced in Pennsylvania and Oregon.
- **1951** The first color TV program was broadcast by CBS (USA).
- **1956** The first practical remote control for television was invented by Robert Adler.
- **1962** The first satellite (Telstar) used to carry TV broadcasts was launched by AT&T.
- **1980s** Video cassette recorder (VCR) became very popular.
- **2000s** DVDs became the major player in home entertainment.
- **2005** Almost all televisions sold were now flat LCD and plasma screens.
- **2006** Blu-Ray DVDs were released in the middle of the year.
- **2009** 3D television sets arrived.
- **2010s** Smart TV becomes popular.

YANCOM/ID/BR

Adapted from https://www.thoughtco.com/the-invention-of-television-1992531; https://bebusinessed.com/history/history-of-the-television/. Accessed on March 10, 2022.

Não escreva no livro.

2. Write in your notebook the sentences that are correct according to the text.

a. Quando começaram a usar satélite em transmissão de TV, a televisão a cabo já tinha sido desenvolvida.

b. 100% dos aparelhos de TV vendidos em 2005 já vinham com tela de plasma e LCD.

c. Antes mesmo do aparecimento do controle remoto, as pessoas já alugavam fitas de vídeo para assistir em casa.

d. Os aparelhos de TV que podem ser conectados à internet apareceram menos de cinco anos após o lançamento do *Blu-Ray*.

3. Answer these questions in your notebook. Explain your answers.

a. É possível saber ao certo em que ano o aparelho de videocassete se tornou popular?

b. Que informação indica ao leitor em que país aconteceu a primeira transmissão em cores?

c. O texto cita os nomes das pessoas e empresas envolvidas em todos os eventos relacionados à história da televisão?

d. Qual informação do texto é uma clara referência a um país da Europa?

e. O texto cita o nome de algum filme relacionado a um dos eventos listados?

Post-reading

1. Talk about these questions with a classmate.

a. In your opinion, which of the inventions related to television you saw here was more important for people in general? Why?

b. Do you think you can find different information about this same topic if you read other texts on the Internet? Why?

c. Can you predict what new things related to television will be invented in the near future?

d. Readers have different opinions about the same text. Choose a word you can use to describe the text you read here: boring / interesting / complicated / useless / too technical. Why do you think so?

Quick quiz – Let's talk!

After spending many hours watching TV, Mike fell asleep and spent the whole night in the sofa. In the morning, his father woke him up saying, "Get up, Mike. It's 10 to seven". He got up immediately and said, "In whose favor?".
According to this joke, what kind of TV show was Mike watching when he fell asleep?

cartoon • sports • musical

Rubberball/Getty Images

Não escreva no livro.

Words, words, words

TV programs

1. Which of these words and expressions do you know? Talk about some of these TV shows with a classmate.

cartoon	film	sports program	series/sitcom
the news	talk show	reality show	music program
soap opera	quiz show	documentary	cooking program

2. In your notebook, label these eight pictures choosing words and expressions from activity 1.

Pietro D'Aprano/Getty Images

Marlene Bergamo/Folhapress

FOX Image Collection/Getty Images

Theo Wargo/NBC/Getty Images

Jaime Trueblood/The CW/Everett/Fotoarena

Yasuyoshi Chiba/AFP

Pendleton Ward/Cartoon Network/Easypix

© Lucasfilm Ltd/ID/BR

3. Match three of the TV shows in activity 1 to the definitions below. Write the answers in your notebook.

a. In this type of TV show, we learn how to prepare a particular food.

b. In this type of TV show, we learn about certain events involving real people. There is a narrator explaining the facts.

c. In this type of TV show, we watch events related to tennis, basketball, football, etc.

No Brasil, chamamos de "novela" os dramas vividos por personagens na TV. Nos Estados Unidos, usa-se o termo *soap opera* (ópera de sabão). Faça uma pesquisa para saber por que eles usam essa expressão para se referir à novela.

Claudio Chyio/ID/BR

Não escreva no livro.

Film genres

1. Read this excerpt from the synopsis of the film *Central Station*. Which film genre do you think it fits into? Answer in your notebook.

Nasared/Shutterstock.com/ID/BR

Photo12.com/AFP

The film centers on a young boy (Vinicius de Oliveira) whose mother is killed in front of Rio de Janeiro's Central Station. Homeless and with nowhere to turn, he is reluctantly befriended by a lonely and cynical woman (Montenegro). Resisting her initial impulse to make a quick profit off the child, she commits to returning him to his father in Brazil's remote Northeast.

Available at http://www.superfilmes.com.br/v2/filme.php?i=2&c=80. Accessed on March 10, 2022.

a. comedy b. romance c. drama d. horror e. action

2. Read some students' comments and try to find out the film genre he/she is talking about. Choose from the words in activity 1 and from the box below. Answer in your notebook.

sci-fi (science fiction)	musical	cartoon	documentary	thriller	adventure	historical	war	western

Claudio Chyio/ID/BR

a. "It's a great movie! The mystery keeps you interested up to the end."

b. "It was a very nice film about the animals that live in the Amazon rainforest."

c. "I felt a bit afraid of all those vampires and zombies on the screen."

d. "It is a really funny film. We laughed all the time. We had a great time!"

e. "The story is about a boy and a girl who love each other, but can't be together."

f. "It's a story about a group of people who travel to another galaxy. A silly story."

g. "I loved it. They sing and dance all the time. You feel like dancing too."

h. "I thought it was too violent. All they do is to shoot at each other!"

i. "The characters are lovely and the animation is first class!"

3. Talk to a classmate about his or her movie preferences.

A: How do you like comedies / thrillers / cartoons?

B: I love them. / I hate them. / I don't like them so much. / They're ok. / I don't know. I never watch them.

Não escreva no livro.

Grammar bits

Passive voice

1. Read these sentences taken from the *Reading corner* section and, in your notebook, write **T** (True) or **F** (False) for each one.

The word *television* **was used** for the first time in Paris.

Cable television systems **were introduced** in Pennsylvania and Oregon.

Black and white broadcasting experiments **were conducted** by RCA.

The first practical remote control for television **was invented** by Robert Adler.

a. The focus in the sentences in the passive voice is on the actions and not on who or what performed these actions.

b. The names of who or what performed some of the actions are mentioned at the end of the sentences.

c. It is impossible to understand the meaning of the sentences that don't mention the names of who performed the actions.

Making sense

Two of the sentences above were reformulated. Read them and write in your notebook the options that complete the rules below.

RCA conducted **black and white broadcasting experiments.**

Robert Adler invented **the first practical remote control for television.**

a. Na passagem da voz ativa para a voz passiva, o **objeto** da sentença na voz **I** (**passiva** / **ativa**) se torna **sujeito** da sentença na voz **II** (**passiva** / **ativa**).

b. Na passagem da voz ativa para a voz passiva, o verbo ***to be*** entra na formação com o **particípio passado** do verbo **III** (**irregular** / **principal**). Na voz passiva, o ***to be*** é usado no tempo em que estiver o verbo na voz ativa e concorda com o novo **IV** (**objeto** / **sujeito**).

A etiqueta da camiseta que você usa sempre traz uma frase curta na voz passiva. Você já tinha notado isso antes?

Claudio Chyio/ID/BR

STILLFX/Shutterstock.com/ID/BR

2. In your notebook, rewrite the following sentences using the passive voice.

a. James Cameron produced the 3D film *Avatar* in 2009.

b. Assis Chateaubriand founded the first TV station in Brazil in 1950.

c. Rede Globo produced the first Brazilian soap opera in color in 1973.

20th Century Fox/Merchandising/Everett Collection/Fotoarena

Avatar. Direction: James Cameron. USA, 20th Century Fox, 2009.

Não escreva no livro.

Comparative adjectives

1. Look at the highlighted words in these headlines. Then complete the rules in the *Making sense* box.

21 hilarious Turning Red memes that are even **funnier** than the film.

Available at https://www.popbuzz.com/tv-film/news/turning-red-memes/. Accessed on March 15, 2022.

YANCOM/ID/BR

Are books **better** than films?

Available at https://www.kingschester.co.uk/news/bbc-school-reports/books-better-films/#:~:text=Books%20develop%20your%20imagination%2C%20are,and%20have%20more%20job%20opportunities. Accessed on August 24, 2022.

YANCOM/ID/BR

10 Movie Villains That Are **More Interesting** Than The Hero.

Available at https://screenrant.com/movie-villains-more-interesting-than-hero/. Accessed on March 15, 2022.

YANCOM/ID/BR

Making sense

Write in your notebook the correct options and examples from the text in each case.

a. Se o adjetivo for **I** (**curto** / **longo**), usamos a palavra *more* na formação do comparativo. A palavra *more* é usada **II** (**antes** / **depois**) do adjetivo. Quando usamos *more* no comparativo, o adjetivo **III** (**sofre** / **não sofre**) alteração na escrita. Um exemplo no texto é a expressão **IV**.

b. Se o adjetivo for **V** (**curto** / **longo**), o comparativo é formado sem a palavra *more*. Nesse caso, o adjetivo (**sofre** / **não sofre**) alteração na escrita. Um exemplo no texto é a expressão **VI** *than*.

- Adjetivos terminados em consoante -y (*funny*, *scary*, *easy*): troque o y por *i* e acrescente -*er*: *funnier*, *scarier*, *easier*
- Adjetivos terminados em "consoante-vogal-consoante" (*big*, *fat*): dobre a consoante e acrescente -*er*: *bigger*, *fatter*.
- Adjetivos terminados em e (*nice*, *late*, *large*): apenas acrescente -*r*: *nicer*, *later*, *larger*.
- Alguns adjetivos de uma sílaba (*fast*, *old*, *tall*, *cold*): apenas acrescente -*er*: *faster*, *older*, *taller*, *colder*.

Exceptions

good > better

bad > worse

2. Complete the sentences in your notebook using the comparatives of the adjectives in parentheses.

a. Magazines are usually **I** (expensive) than newspapers.

b. Going to the movies is **II** (good) than watching films at home.

c. Ben Stiller is **III** (funny) than Jim Carrey.

d. I think Spanish is **IV** (easy) than Italian.

e. Ana Hickmann is **V** (tall) than Fernanda Lima.

Go to **Grammar reference** (unit 1).

Open your ears

1. Do you know where the films below were made? Look at the countries in the box and make in your notebook a sentence matching them to the corresponding movie poster.

Brazil	France	United States	Mexico

Examples: *Xingu* was made in... / I think *Captain Fantastic* was made in...

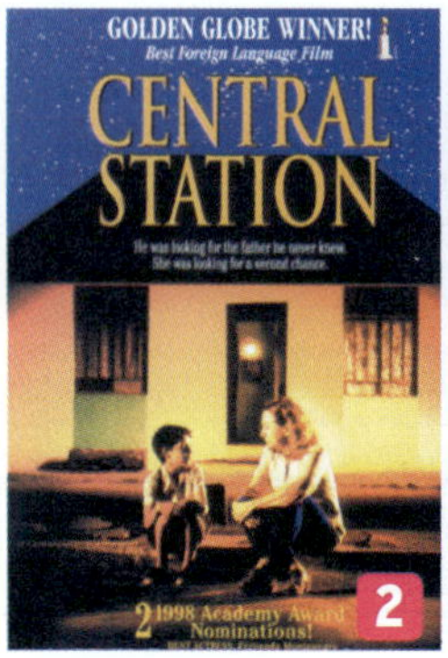

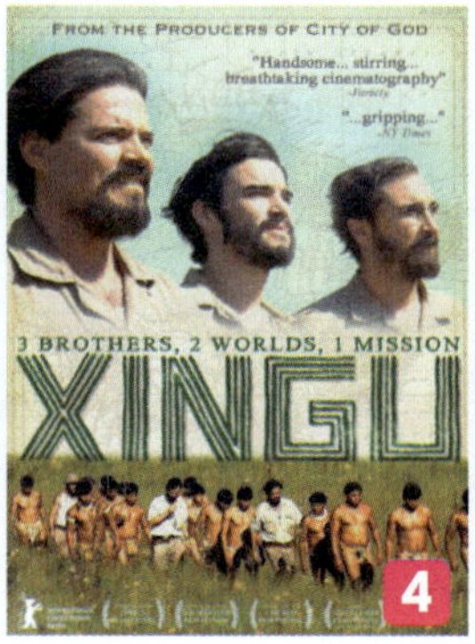

Alebrije Cine y Video/ID/BR; Europa Filmes/ID/BR; Electric City Entertainment ShivHans Pictures/ID/BR; O2 Filmes/Globo Filmes/ID/BR; Fac-símile: ID/BR

2. Read a synopsis of one of the movies above and answer in your notebook: What movie is it?

> Deep in the forests of the Pacific Northwest, isolated from society, a devoted father (Viggo Mortensen) dedicates his life to transforming his six young children into extraordinary adults. But when a tragedy strikes the family, they are forced to leave this self-created paradise and begin a journey into the outside world that challenges his idea of what it means to be a parent and brings into question everything he's taught them.
>
> Available at https://www.rottentomatoes.com/m/captain_fantastic/. Accessed on March 10, 2022.

Nas atividades de *listening*, procure ler as questões antes de ouvir a gravação. Assim, você já terá uma ideia sobre o assunto e saberá em que vai precisar prestar mais atenção. Ao ouvir novamente a gravação, fique bastante atento, mesmo que você já tenha respondido às questões. Sempre vale a pena conferir!

Claudio Chyio/ID/BR

2 3. You are going to listen to Viggo Mortensen talking about how he felt when he read the script of the film for the first time. In your notebook, write the suitable letter-number combination.

a. According to Mortensen, the script made him **A**.

- **I** be awaken and sleepy
- **II** laugh and cry

b. He liked the script because it also made him question **B**.

- **I** his role as a father and a person in society
- **II** his work as an actor

4. Talk about the questions below with a classmate.

a. In your opinion, which of the images in the posters above is more creative or more beautiful?

b. Why do you think the American film industry exports more films than the Brazilian film industry?

Speaker's corner

Conducting a survey on TV watching

1. Suppose you are going to ask some people on the street to answer a survey. What kind of language can you use to start and finish the conversation?

Please, please, answer this survey. / Hey, answer this survey for me. / Excuse me, I'm doing a survey on TV. May I ask you some questions? / That's all, that's all. Now you can leave. / That's all. Thanks for your attention. Goodbye. / I liked your answers... Congratulations.

2. Use the questionnaire below to interview a classmate and write his answers in your notebook.

1. How often do you watch TV?

a. Every day. b. 3-6 days a week. c. Less than 3 days a week.

2. When do you usually watch TV?

a. In the morning.
b. In the afternoon.
c. In the evening.
d. Late at night.

3. Do you like watching...?

I like II don't mind III dislike

a. the news
b. soap operas
c. talk shows
d. documentaries
e. quiz shows
f. series
g. films
h. reality shows
i. cartoons
j. sports programs

4. Which channel do you like the best?

5. Do you like watching TV alone or with your family?

6. Could you live without TV for a week?

7. Do you think that TV makes people lazy?

8. Do you think there is too much violence on TV?

3. Get together with three other students. Compare and discuss your results. Can you come to any conclusions?

4. In your notebook, write a paragraph about the results and the conclusions of your survey. Look at this example.

I found out that most people watch TV every day. They usually watch TV in the evening. Most people like watching... The TV channel most people like the best is...

Não escreva no livro.

Pen to paper

Writing a film review

Pre-writing

1. In your opinion, which information is essential in a film review? Why? Discuss with your classmates about it.

2. Look at what a reviewer has written about this film. Then, read the four questions that follow and, in your notebook, answer **Yes** or **No**.

Peter Mountain/Warner Bros/Album/Fotoarena

Charlie and the chocolate factory. Direction: Tim Burton. USA, Warner Bros, 2005.

Everything about *Charlie and the chocolate factory* is awesome. Johnny Depp takes on one of his most ambitious roles yet as Willy Wonka, creating a really eccentric character. Each set has its own unique look and a lot of it was made by hand and not computer. Special effects were of course used, especially when filming the Oompa Loompas. If you see one movie this summer it should be *Charlie and the chocolate factory*. Everyone will love it. It may not be the best movie to take really small kids to, though. Johnny Depp's performance is amazing, but his character can be a bit creepy at times.

Adapted from http://www.kidzworld.com/article/5819-charlie-and-the-chocolate-factory-dvd-review. Accessed on March 10, 2022.

a. Is the writer enthusiastic about the film?

b. Does the writer tell about the director?

c. Does the writer mention the main actor?

d. Does the writer recommend the film?

Dictionary 3

eccentric *noun* UK /ɪk'sen.trɪk/ US /ɪk'sen.trɪk/

Definition: strange or unusual, sometimes in a humorous way.

Available at https://dictionary.cambridge.org/dictionary/english/eccentric. Accessed on March 10, 2022.

Follow these steps to write your film review

1. Choose a film that you have watched. It may be a film that you have enjoyed or not. Search information about the film: Who directed it? Who are the protagonists? Is the film based on a book? Make a list in your notebook.

2. Based on the plot of the film, performance of the actors, special effects, etc., think about your opinion about it: Did you like the film? Is it good / bad / funny / sad? What are the positive and the negative aspects of the film?

3. Write in your notebook the review of the film you have chosen. Try to use adjectives and interesting vocabulary. Remember that your goal is to have many people reading your text.

Focus on culture

Movies and culture

Why do movie titles in Spain end up with such strange translations?

Two Hollywood films, *La La Land* and *Zootopia*, have just landed in Spanish cinemas with rather puzzling name changes. Although the average Spanish movie goer is probably able to pronounce and remember the original titles, in Spain the pair have been rendered as *La ciudad de las estrellas* (or *The city of stars*) and *Zootrópolis* respectively. The renaming may seem superfluous, but some experts say they are necessary.

In the musical *La La Land*, Ryan Gosling and Emma Stone fall in love while dreaming of making it big in Los Angeles. The title is a play-on-words that even an advanced student of English might miss. To be in "La La Land" means to be detached from reality, a state in which the film's protagonists often find themselves, especially during the musical numbers. At the same time, 'La La' is a reduplication of Los Angeles' initials – L.A. – which is often how people refer to the city that is home to Hollywood. [...]

A haunting song entitled *City of Stars*, composed by Justin Hurwitz, is used throughout the film. The song's title is another nod to Los Angeles, yet more comprehensible to the Spanish audience than La La Land. This explains the marketers' decision to call the movie *La ciudad de las estrellas* (*The City of Stars*) in Spain. [...]

Spain was not the only country that had to adapt the title [...]. In Brazil, it's called *La La Land: Cantando Estações* (or, *La La Land: Singing Seasons*); in countries such as Mexico, Argentina and Peru it is *La La Land: Una historia de amor* (*La La Land: A love story*); in Portugal it is *La La Land: Melodia de Amor* (*La La Land: Melody of Love*); and for the francophone audience in Canada, it has been distributed as *Pour l'amour d'Hollywood* (*For the love of Hollywood*).

La La Land was made by Universal Pictures, a multinational company that has a presence in nearly all the world's markets. For every movie they release, there is a global strategy. At Universal Pictures, translating movie titles "makes up part of our everyday work," said a spokesperson from the company's Spanish division.

Héctor Llanos Martínez. *El País*. Available at https://elpais.com/elpais/2017/02/01/inenglish/1485965463_990505.html. Accessed on March 10, 2022.

1. Read the text and talk to your classmates about these questions.
   a. What is the text about?
   b. According to the text, "The renaming may seem superfluous, but some experts say they are necessary." Do you agree with that? Why (not)?

2. In the world of entertainment, sometimes cultural adaptations are as important as language translations. In groups, do some research on how some games, films and cartoons were adapted to fit foreign public. Create a poster to show what you have found out.

Self-assessment

Reflect about your own learning

assessment | learning | reflect | autonomy | English | responsibility | feedback

Freepik/ID/BR

I do it with confidence.	I do it well.	I can get better.

1. Como você avalia seu aprendizado nesta unidade? Reflita.

a. Que parte da unidade (seção, texto, imagem, mensagem do tutor, etc.) mais lhe agradou? Por quê?

b. Qual foi a parte de que você menos gostou? Por quê?

c. Você se lembra de alguma coisa que viu nesta unidade e que o ajudou fora da aula de inglês?

2. O que você pode fazer para melhorar seu aprendizado de inglês? Observe as opções abaixo e pense a respeito delas.

- Ler mais.
- Fazer mais atividades.
- Solucionar dúvidas com o professor.
- Trocar ideias com os colegas.
- Ouvir músicas em inglês.
- Assistir a filmes em inglês com legendas.

Syda Productions/Shutterstock.com/ID/BR

Não escreva no livro.

UNIT

2 Famous people

In this unit you will talk about being famous and do activities that present the names of different jobs. The main text focuses on the lives of two people who became famous worldwide when they were young. All over the unit you will be engaged in activities that feature the following elements:

- **Genre:** biography
- **Vocabulary:** jobs and careers
- **Grammar:** relative pronouns; superlative adjectives

Quick challenge

Read the questions below. Scan the pages of this unit and write the answers in your notebook.

a. Who is the famous person in the *Speaker's corner* section?

b. What section is the picture with several boys singing in?

c. Which page is the photo of a man who created famous cartoons?

d. One of these pictures is not used in this unit. Which one?

1

Pratik Chorge/Hindustan Times/Getty Images

3
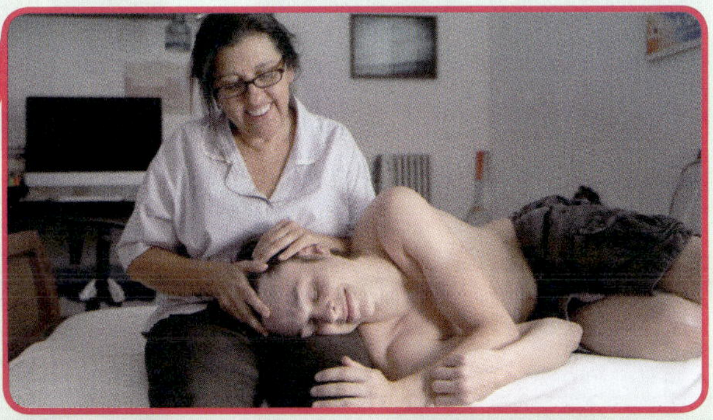
Oscilloscope Laboratories/Everett Collection/Fotoarena

2

Bettmann/Corbis/Getty Images

4

Clément Mahoudeau/AFP/Getty Images

Não escreva no livro.

A first approach

Talking about the topic

1

Clément Mahoudeau/AFP/Getty Images

2

Dominique Charriau/WireImage/Getty Images

3

Chris Pizzello/Invision/AP

4

David M. Benett/Dave Benett/Getty Images

5

Image Press Agency/Alamy/Fotoarena

6

Pascal Le Segretain/Getty Images

7

Delmiro Junior/Shutterstock.com/ID/BR

8

Independent Photo Agency/Alamy/Fotoarena

1. What do you know about the people in the pictures? For example, their names, their careers, their professions, their birthplaces, etc.
2. Do you think they live a normal life? Why (not)?
3. In your opinion, what are the advantages and disadvantages of being famous?

Exploring the topic

1. These sentences refer to six images on the previous page. Match each sentence to the corresponding picture and write the combination in your notebook.

A She is a pop singer. She was born in Barbados.

B She is one of the most famous fashion models in the world.

C He featured the song "Peaches" with Justin Bieber, which was released on 2021.

D She is a pop singer. She is one of the most popular and best-selling Brazilian female singers.

E He is one of the most popular Brazilian soccer players.

F She is a famous American singer, performer, songwriter and actress. She has won 28 Grammy Awards.

2. Write in your notebook the option that is true for you.

a. I would not like to be famous.

b. I would like to be famous as a/an:

singer	TV actor/actress	writer	model	dancer
TV host	movie star	journalist	musician	environmental activist
painter	scientist	football player	politician	teacher
doctor	basketball player	playwright	movie director	

3. Add one more picture to the "Hall of Fame". In your notebook, draw or glue the picture of a famous person in your own community and write something about him/her.

Looking around

1. Who are some of the "famous people" in your region? Why are they popular?
2. Would you like to take part in a reality show? Why (not)?
3. Why do you think many people want to become famous?

Não escreva no livro.

Reading corner

Pre-reading

1. Use some of these sentences and words to answer the questions about the texts 1 and 2.

Preface. | Not mentioned. | In New York City. | On March 1st, 1994. | On a specific website. | Justin Bieber. | In a tabloid. | Email message. | In a chat room. | Biography.

a. Which word best describes this type of text?

b. Where were these texts posted on?

c. When were these texts published?

d. Who produced these texts?

Text 1

Justin Bieber

Born on March 1, 1994, in Ontario, Canada. Justin Bieber was raised by a single mom in the small town of Stratford. Bieber went from an unknown, untrained singer to a budding superstar with a big-time record deal after his mother posted YouTube clips of her boy performing, all within just two years. His debut album *My World* hit stores in November 2009, is a true overnight success.

Bieber always had an interest in music. His mother gave him a drum kit for his second birthday and, as he tells it, he was "basically banging on everything I could get my hands on".

Kevin Mazur/AMA2020/Getty Images

But it was an obscure talent contest in his hometown, in which the 12-year-old Bieber finished second, that put him on the road to superstardom. As a way to share his singing with family, Justin and his mom began posting clips of Bieber performing covers of Stevie Wonder, Michael Jackson, and Ne-Yo on YouTube.

Within months, Justin was an Internet sensation, with a large following of fans, and an eager manager arranging for the teenager to fly to Atlanta to consider a record deal. There, Bieber had a chance meeting with Usher, who eventually signed the young singer to a contract.

Adapted from https://www.biography.com/musician/justin-bieber. Accessed on March 15, 2022.

Não escreva no livro.

Text 2

Macaulay Culkin

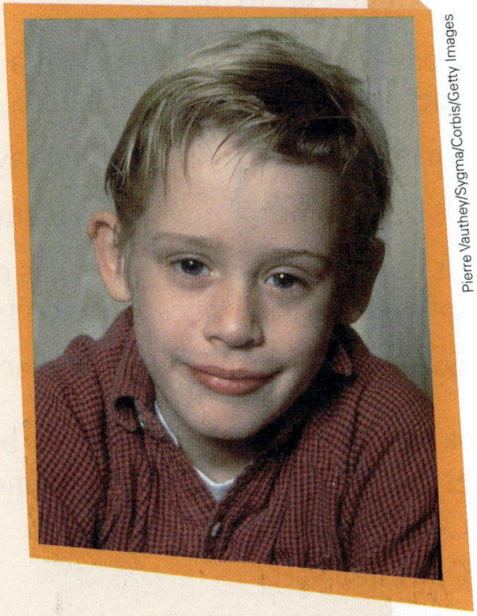

Pierre Vauthey/Sygma/Corbis/Getty Images

[...] Macaulay Carson Culkin was born on August 26, 1980, in New York City. The third of seven children, Culkin was drawn to the limelight from a young age. He performed in his first play Off-Broadway at age four. Culkin studied the performing arts extensively as a child, including training at Balanchine's School of the American Ballet, and appeared in numerous television commercials.

[...] Culkin made his feature screen debut in 1988's *Rocket Gibraltar*, but it was his charming turn as John Candy's precocious nephew in 1989's comedic hit *Uncle Buck* that made him Hollywood's favorite child actor. His stardom hit meteoric proportions the following year when he starred in the wildly successful holiday comedy *Home Alone*. The film was the highest-grossing film of the year and spawned a slightly less successful sequel, *Home Alone 2: Lost in New York* in 1992.

In 1991, Macaulay Culkin impressed audiences and critics with his heartfelt and endearing performance as the best friend of a troubled young girl in the tear-jerker *My Girl*. Subsequent films, including 1993's *The Good Son* and 1994's *Richie Rich* were underwhelming and emphasized Culkin's waning popularity. [...]

Available at https://www.biography.com/actor/macaulay-culkin. Accessed on March 17, 2022.

Dictionary 4

spawn *verb* UK /spɔːn/ US /spɑːn/

Definition: to cause something new, or many new things, to grow or start suddenly.

Available at https://dictionary.cambridge.org/dictionary/english/spawn. Accessed on May 2, 2022.

Quando lemos uma biografia, queremos conhecer a vida de alguém. Mas não dá para dizer que o conteúdo ali é 100% verdadeiro, não é? Temos de checar se o autor da biografia tem simpatia pelo biografado, se conversou com ele ou apenas leu outros textos sobre sua vida. O leitor crítico é aquele que, além de desfrutar da leitura, leva em conta também quem escreveu, para quem escreveu, quem está patrocinando o livro, etc.

Claudio Chiyo/ID/BR

Não escreva no livro.

Exploring the text

1. Read the statements below. Then, in your notebook, write **T** (True) or **F** (False) for each one of them.

   a. É possível constatar que um dos artistas nasceu há mais tempo que o outro apenas observando o tipo de foto.

   b. Um dos textos não apresenta palavras relacionadas ao mundo digital.

   c. Os dois textos trazem muitos exemplos de verbos de ação no passado.

   d. Os dois textos mencionam títulos de trabalhos dos artistas, mas um deles não informa o ano de lançamento do trabalho.

   e. Só um dos textos menciona a relação do artista com um membro da família.

2. Look at these fragments from the biographies. Write in your notebook the ones that express the writer's opinion about some facts.

I Justin Bieber	II Macaulay Culkin
A for his second birthday	J The third of seven children
B all in just two years	K was born on August 26, 1980
C hit stores in November 2009	L charming turn as John Candy's precocious nephew
D an Internet sensation	M Hollywood's favorite child actor
E big-time record deal	N His stardom hit meteoric proportions
F true overnight success	O the wildly successful holiday comedy
G began posting clips	P slightly less successful sequel
H obscure talent contest	Q his feature screen debut in 1988
I eager manager	R impressed audiences and critics

3. Look at the different ways the writer refers to Macaulay Culkin in the text. Do the same with Justin Bieber's text. Answer in your notebook.

   Macaulay Culkin - he - Macaulay Carson Culkin - Culkin.

Post-reading

1. Talk about these questions with a classmate.

   a. In your opinion, which artist has or had the most interesting career? Why?

   b. Which information about these two artists interested you most? Why?

   c. Why are some people famous when they are young and lose their popularity when they grow up?

Words, words, words

Jobs and careers

1. Do you remember what these people do? Match every name to its corresponding occupation and write the combination in your notebook.

Javier Bragado/Redferns/Getty Images

Daniel Caesar (2019)

I Emma Watson is...	IV Neymar is...
II Adriana Lima is...	V Rihanna is...
III Daniel Caesar is...	VI Far From Alaska is...

A a singer.	D a singer and songwriter.
B an actress.	E a soccer player.
C a model.	F a group of musicians.

2. In your notebook, create a table with the following categories. Then, relate the careers below to the appropriate column. Follow the model.

Television/Movies	Music	Sports/Fitness	Fashion
actress	musician	soccer player	model

actor	costume designer	make-up artist	personal trainer
artist manager	director	massage therapist	photographer
basketball player	DJ	dressmaker	record producer
camera operator	editor	music promoter	referee
coach	gym instructor	sound technician	singer
conductor	hair artist	nutritionist	stylist

3. In your notebook, complete each sentence below using at least two careers presented in activities 1 and 2.

a. Careers which are common among the people in my community: I.

b. Careers which are not common among the people in my community: II.

4. Search other careers and jobs in different areas to present next class. There are some areas you can choose: health / education / agriculture / science / Internet / car industry. You can also use your family members' occupations and do some research about it to present in English. Write in your notebook.

Não escreva no livro.

Grammar bits

Relative pronouns

1. Read two sentences that appeared in the previous sections. Answer the questions in your notebook.

A There, Bieber had a chance meeting with Usher, **who** eventually signed the young singer to a contract.

Is the word **who** referring to Justin Bieber or to the singer Usher?

B He featured the song "Peaches" with Justin Bieber, **which** was released on 2021.

Is the word **which** referring to Justin Bieber or to the song "Peaches"?

Making sense

Complete these rules according to the examples in the sentences above. Use your notebook.

a. When we refer to things, ideas, concepts or animals, we use the relative pronoun **I**. There is one example in sentence **II**.

b. When we refer to people, we use the relative pronoun **III**. There is one example in sentence **IV**.

Claudio Chiyo/ID/BR

Em alguns casos, o pronome relativo *that* pode substituir *who* e *which*. Você pode dizer, por exemplo: *Daniel Caesar is the singer* **that (who)** *featured the song "Peaches" with Justin Bieber.* E pode dizer também: *The song* **that (which)** *Daniel Caesar featured with Justin Bieber was "Peaches".*

2. Look at this other example and write in your notebook the appropriate answer.

Bieber, **whose** debut album *My World* hit stores in November 2009, is a true overnight success.

A palavra destacada equivale, em português, a:

a. que. b. quem. c. cujo. d. o qual.

3. Match the words on the left to the corresponding actions on the right. Then, write in your notebook the appropriate combination of letters-numbers.

A	cameras	I	cut things
B	carpenters	II	connect one computer to another secretly and often illegally
C	chefs	III	give us milk
D	hackers	IV	write for newspapers
E	cows	V	take pictures
F	journalists	VI	make furniture out of wood
G	scissors	VII	repair cars
H	mechanics	VIII	cook in a restaurant

4. Now, in your notebook, complete these definitions and don't forget to use **who**, **whose**, or **which**. Make the necessary changes to the verbs. Follow the example.

A camera is a machine which takes pictures.

a. A carpenter is someone **I** job is to **II**.

b. A chef is someone **III**.

c. A hacker is someone **IV**.

d. A cow is an animal **V**.

e. A journalist is someone **VI**.

f. A scissors is an object **VII**.

g. A mechanic is someone **VIII**.

Superlative adjectives

1. Read these sentences taken from a website and complete the *Making sense* box. Write the appropriate option in your notebook.

ID/BR

Shirley Temple was easily the most popular and famous child star of all time. [...]

At age six she was the youngest presenter at the Oscars ever. She presented the "Best Actress" award in 1935. [...]

2005: Premiere Magazine ranked her as #33 on a list of the Greatest Movie Stars of All Time [...].

Bettmann/Corbis/Getty Images

Adapted from http://www.imdb.com/name/nm0000073/bio. Accessed on March 15, 2022.

Making sense

1. O superlativo é usado quando comparamos uma coisa a **I** (**outra coisa** / **várias coisas**).

2. Se o adjetivo for **II** (**curto** / **longo**), usamos *the most* na formação do superlativo. O adjetivo é usado sempre **III** (**antes** / **depois**) de *the most*.

3. Quando usamos *the most* no superlativo, o adjetivo **IV** (**sofre** / **não sofre**) alteração na escrita.

4. Se o adjetivo for **V** (**curto** / **longo**), o superlativo é formado sem *the most* Nesse caso, o adjetivo **VI** (**sofre** / **não sofre**) alteração na escrita. Ele recebe a terminação **VII** (**-er** / **-est**) e é precedido do artigo *the*.

- Adjetivos terminados em **consoante-y** (*funny*, *scary*, *easy*): troque o **y** por ***i*** e acrescente **-est**: ***funniest***, ***scariest***, ***easiest***.
- Adjetivos terminados em "**consoante-vogal-consoante**" (***big***, ***fat***): dobre a consoante final e acrescente **-est**: *biggest*, *fattest*.
- Adjetivos terminados em **e** (*nice*, *late*, *large*): apenas acrescente **–st**: *nicest*, *latest*, *largest*.
- Outros casos de adjetivos de uma sílaba (*fast*, *old*, *tall*, *cold*, *young*): apenas acrescente **–est**: *fastest*, *oldest*, *tallest*, *coldest*, *youngest*.

2. Look back at Macaulay Culkin's biography on page 27. Find one case of superlative and copy the sentence in your notebook.

Exceptions
good > the best
bad > the worst

3. In your notebook, complete the sentences using the superlative form of the adjectives in the box.

large	funny	good	hard	famous
	bad	talented	amazing	

a. The Vienna Choir Boys is **I** boy's choir in the world.

b. Many people consider Pelé as **II** football player ever.

c. The Amazon River is probably **III** river in the world.

d. Many actors say that Hamlet is one of **IV** characters to play in the theater.

e. Michael Jackson was definitely **V** artist in his family.

f. Walt Disney created some of **VI** cartoons in the movies.

g. I think that Justin Bieber's latest song is **VII** he recorded so far.

h. In my opinion, Aziz Ansari is **VIII** actor in Hollywood movies.

Pratik Chorge/Hindustan Times/Getty Images

The Vienna Choir Boys, 2013.

O superlativo usado com mais frequência no cotidiano é o de superioridade. É mais comum dizer, por exemplo, *the most famous actress* do que *the least famous actress*. O superlativo de inferioridade em inglês tem a seguinte formação: *the least* + adjetivo. Exemplos: *Mike is the least tall in the class. | This is the l east comfortable bed in the house.*

Claudio Chiyo/ID/BR

Go to **Grammar reference** (unit 2).

Não escreva no livro.

Open your ears

1. Careers game. You have one minute to make in your notebook a list of as many occupations as you can remember in English. When the time is up, your teacher will say STOP!

5 **2.** Listen to the song about professions and answer the following questions in your notebook.

Macrovector/Shutterstock.com/ID/BR

a. Write at least five professions you heard in the song.

b. Which of these careers **are not** mentioned in the conversation?

banker	astronaut	taxi driver	photographer
firefighter	dentist	web designer	baseball player
dancer	nurse	engineer	teacher

c. Discuss with a classmate which of these professions you like most and which one you don't think that is a good choice for you. Explain the reasons why.

d. What about you? Do you know what you want to be when you are older?

Discussion point

- Para exercer algumas profissões, é necessário ter cursado o Ensino Superior. Há algum caso assim nas profissões apresentadas nesta atividade? Você acha correta essa exigência?
- Em sua opinião, por que algumas pessoas não dão continuidade aos estudos após o Ensino Médio?

Dictionary 6

firefighter *noun* UK /ˈfaɪəˌfaɪ.təʳ/ US /ˈfaɪrˌfaɪ.t̬ɚ/

Definition: a person whose job is to stop fires from burning.

Available at http://dictionary.cambridge.org/dictionary/british/firefighter?q=firefighter. Accessed on March 15, 2022.

Não escreva no livro.

Speaker's corner

Interviewing a celebrity

1. Read this short biography about a very famous person worldwide.

Edson Arantes do Nascimento, most commonly known by his nickname "Pelé", was born in Três Corações, Minas Gerais, Brazil, in 1940. He grew up in poverty in Bauru, São Paulo. He earned extra money by working in tea shops as a servant. Taught to play by his coach, he could not afford a proper football and usually played with a sock stuffed with newspaper, tied with a string. In 1954, aged fourteen, he joined Bauru Athletic Club Juniors. In 1956, Pelé was taken to Santos, an industrial and port city in the state of São Paulo, to try out for professional club Santos Futebol Clube. It was said at the time that the 15-year-old would be "the greatest football player in the world".

Adapted from http://en.wikipedia.org/wiki/Pel%C3%A9. Accessed on March 15, 2022.

Arquivo/Estadão Conteúdo

Pelé, 1958.

2. Now you will interview Pelé! Based on the text, write in your notebook questions for these answers. Follow the example.

   a. It's Edson Arantes do Nascimento. What's your real name?
   b. My nickname is Pelé.
   c. I was born in Três Corações, Minas Gerais, in Brazil.
   d. No, I didn't. Actually I grew up in a city called Bauru, in São Paulo.
   e. Oh, I played it with a sock stuffed with newspaper. I was really poor.
   f. I was fourteen.
   g. I went to Santos in 1956.

3. Work in pairs. Student A plays the interviewer and Student B plays Pelé. Memorize your parts and act out the dialogue.

4. Still in pairs, prepare another interview. Follow these guidelines.

   a. Choose a celebrity to interview. It can be someone you know well or a person you want to know more about. You can also choose to interview an imaginary celebrity. In this case, use your creativity.
   b. Write in your notebook at least five questions to ask during the interview. Then, write the answers. If you have doubts, ask your teacher.
   c. Rehearse the interview. Memorize your lines. When you are ready, present your "talk show" to your classmates.

Claudio Chiyo/ID/BR

As perguntas que formulamos para o roteiro de uma entrevista oral às vezes soam artificiais, pois elas são apenas um guia. É na hora da entrevista em si que improvisações e marcas de oralidade vão surgindo, como *Oh, really? Cool!* e *You're kidding!*. Hesitações também costumam ocorrer, pois nem sempre o entrevistado tem as respostas "na ponta da língua".

Pen to paper

Writing a short biography

Pre-writing

1. The reasons that make people read biographies vary a lot. Choose from the options below one or two reasons you think are most common and copy them in your noteboook.

just for curiosity | to write a screenplay (for a film) | to do a school project | to write a play (theater) | to know what to do to have professional success

2. The sentences below make up a short biography of Walt Disney. They are in the wrong order here. Organize the text in your notebook, putting these sentences in chronological order. The first sentence is given to you.

Walt Disney was born in Chicago on December 5th, 1901.

J. R. Eyerman/Time Life Pictures/Getty Images

Walt Disney.

A Many of his first drawings as a child were of farm animals.

B In 1928 he created Mickey Mouse, his most famous cartoon character. That was the start of Disney's amazing success.

C In 1920, he joined the Kansas City Ad Company, where he made cartoon advertisements.

D Walt Disney died at the age of 65 on December 15th, 1966.

E He was one of five children and grew up on a farm in Missouri.

F He won many awards for his films, which include *Snow White and the Seven Dwarfs*, *Bambi* and *Pinocchio*.

G Disney's ambition, though, was to make films, so in 1923 he decided to go to Hollywood.

H At the age of sixteen, Disney returned to Chicago where he studied art.

I His greatest creation, however, was Disneyland, which opened in 1955 in California.

Source: Virginia Evans and Jenny Dooley. *Reading & Writing Targets 2.* Swansea: Express Publishing, 1998.

Não escreva no livro.

3. In your notebook, organize the sentences from the previous page in four paragraphs.
   a. Paragraph 1
   b. Paragraph 2
   c. Paragraph 3
   d. Paragraph 4
4. Now, in your notebook, copy the sentences according to the sequence that you have decided above.

Follow these steps to write the biography of a famous person

1. Copy the items below in your notebook and use them as a guide to take notes related to the person you are going to write about. Remember to use only short sentences or keywords. This is not the text of the biography yet. These are only notes to be developed later.

Name	His/her adolescence	His/her achievements
His/her birth	His/her birthplace	His/her death (?)
His/her childhood	Beginning of his/her work life	His/her goals

2. In your notebook, write the biography of the person you have chosen. Use the short biography on the previous page and the texts in the *Reading corner* section as a reference.
3. For better results, write the biography in different stages. Start by collecting information. Then, choose the necessary vocabulary and organize the paragraphs. Note that some biographies are written in the Simple present, but they still refer to the past. Use your notebook.
4. In your notebook, write a first version of your text and ask your classmates and teacher to read it and give you feedback.
5. Write another version based on the feedback you have received.

Quick quiz – Let's talk!

1. Walt Disney created characters that became popular all over the world. In Brazil, the character called "Goofy" became popular as:
   Donald • Pateta • Tio Patinhas
2. The character called "Scrooge McDuck" became popular in Brazil as:
   Tio Patinhas • Donald • Pateta

Que tal juntar todos os textos dos colegas e organizar um pequeno livro de biografias? Use os recursos eletrônicos e sua imaginação!

Claudio Chiyo/ID/BR

Não escreva no livro.

Focus on culture

Reframing the presidential portrait

1. Read the text below with attention and talk to your classmates about the following questions.

'A Game Changer.' How a Painting of President Obama Broke the Rules

Saul Loeb/AFP

Former US President Barack Obama and First Lady Michelle Obama stand before their portraits and respective artists, Kehinde Wiley (left) and Amy Sherald (right), after an unveiling at the Smithsonian's National Portrait Gallery in Washington, D.C., on Feb. 12, 2018.

For the first time in its 56-year history, the National Portrait Gallery commissioned two African-American artists, Kehinde Wiley and Amy Sherald, to paint the First Couple.

The Obamas chose Wiley and Sherald after considering portfolios of some 20 artists. The Obamas interviewed a few at the White House, but ultimately decided on the two contemporary portraitists with whom they each felt a connection. [...]

"The way we think about a presidential portrait is one that is imbued with dignity from the outset. It is a vocabulary that has been fixed. The challenge here was move forward with a different type of narrative", says Wiley. The artist stripped away the trappings of office in order to depict the former President's life journey. African blue lilies are a nod to Obama's father's home country of Kenya. Chrysanthemums are the official flower of the city of Chicago, where Obama met his wife Michelle and started both his family and political career. Pikake, or Arabian jasmine, thrives in Hawaii, where the President spent much of his youth. [...] The way the president appears to lean toward the viewer, his collar unbuttoned, exudes a level of openness not seen in some of the other portraits.

In Sherald's portrait, the former First Lady's silvery skin glows against a pale blue backdrop. Where Wiley's piece is exuberant and lush, Sherald's is spare, casting the First Lady as the focus. The singularity of the piece asks the viewer to contemplate the strength and presence of Michelle Obama both as she was in the White House, and as she remains in the hearts of the many who look up to her.

While there has been a widespread embrace of the uniqueness of the artwork, many will be challenged by their unconventional nature. To really see them, says an art specialist, will require the viewer to think about portraiture in a fresh way.

Adapted from http://time.com/5158961/obama-portrait-kehinde-wiley-amy-sherald-interview/. Accessed on March 15, 2022.

a. According to the text, why are these portraits game changers?

b. Did you like the official portraits of the Obama couple? Why (not)?

2. It's your turn! Make a portrait of someone famous which depicts some elements of his/her journey. Then, show it to your classmates and ask for their feedback.

Self-assessment

Reflect about your own learning

assessment | learning | reflect | autonomy

English | responsibility | feedback

Freepik/ID/BR

I do it with confidence.	I do it well.	I can get better.

1. Como você avalia seu aprendizado nesta unidade? Reflita.

   a. Que parte da unidade (seção, texto, imagem, mensagem do tutor, etc.) mais lhe agradou? Por quê?

   b. Qual foi a parte de que você menos gostou? Por quê?

   c. Você se lembra de alguma coisa que viu nesta unidade e que o ajudou fora da aula de inglês?

2. O que você pode fazer para melhorar seu aprendizado de inglês? Observe as opções abaixo e pense a respeito delas.

- Ler mais.
- Fazer mais atividades.
- Solucionar suas dúvidas com o professor.
- Trocar ideias com os colegas.
- Ouvir músicas em inglês.
- Assistir a filmes em inglês com legendas.

Sirikorn Thamniyom/Shutterstock.com/ID/BR

Não escreva no livro.

UNIT 3

People who make a difference

In this unit you will get to know a little bit about doing volunteer work to help other people in our community. The main text presents some ideas to help us choose what kind of volunteer work we could do. All over the unit you will be engaged in activities that feature the following elements:

- **Genres:** speech; online form
- **Vocabulary:** qualities of a good volunteer
- **Grammar:** modal verbs

Quick challenge

Read the questions below. Scan the pages of this unit and write the answers in your notebook.

a. What is the name of the song in the *Open your ears* section?

b. Look at the picture of this girl. Who is she?

Carlos Caetano/Shutterstock.com/ID/BR

c. One of these pictures is not used in this unit. Which one?

1

Sabrina Eras/ID/BR

3

Africa Studio/Shutterstock.com/ID/BR

2

Pakhnyushcha/Shutterstock.com/ID/BR

4

Rawpixel.com/Shutterstock.com/ID/BR

Não escreva no livro.

A first approach

Talking about the topic

1

Africa Studio/Shutterstock.com/ID/BR

4

Hero Images/Getty Images

2

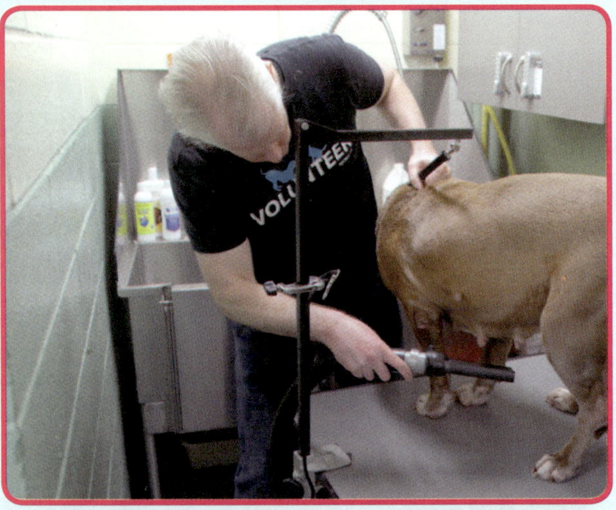

Yasser Suoisri/Future Publishing/Getty Images

5

Monkey Business Images/Shutterstock.com/ID/BR

3

Patrick Van Katwijk/Getty Images

6

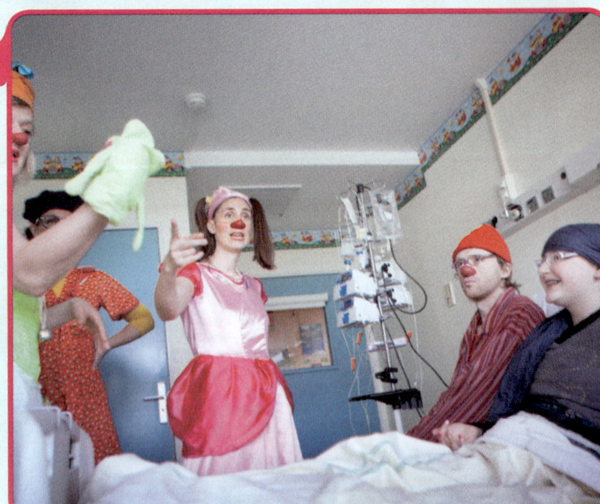

BSIP/Universal Images Group/Getty Images

Não escreva no livro.

1. What do you know about the word that appears in picture 1?

2. In your opinion, what is the relationship among the people in each of the images on the previous page?

3. Do you think these are real life scenes or settings specially created by the photographers?

Exploring the topic

1. What can people do to contribute to society? In your notebook, match five of these types of volunteer work to five pictures in this section.

   A Visit a hospital to provide comfort, encouragement, and support for patients.

   B Teach computer skills to children and teenagers.

   C Offer part of your time to visit a home for senior citizens and talk to them, read stories, or just listen to them.

   D Make some sandwiches and soup to distribute to hungry homeless people.

   E Dedicate part of your time to care for homeless dogs and cats in your community.

   F Donate food, clothing, and other items to victims of catastrophes.

   G Help teachers in your community with recreational activities for children and teenagers.

   H Support or take part in campaigns to help protect wildlife and natural areas.

   I Provide safe transportation for people who need to see the doctor or go to other personal appointments.

2. Which of the types of volunteer work in activity 1 can be done by teenagers? Discuss it with your classmates.

Looking around

1. Do you know people who do volunteer work in your own community? What do they do?

2. Do you think that 100% of the people who do volunteer work are really concerned about helping?

3. How do you interpret this image? Do you think everybody interprets it the same way?

Pakhnyushcha/Shutterstock.com/ID/BR

Reading corner

Pre-reading

1. Read what two people say about volunteering. Then, tell a classmate how much you agree with them.

Carlos Caetano/Shutterstock.com/ID/BR

Ainsley: I feel incredibly fortunate to have had the opportunity to live and teach at TYS. Never again will I be so lucky to work with students with such a thirst for knowledge and a desire to develop their skills. Top this off with the most beautiful seaside location in Ghana and a handful of like-minded volunteers, teachers and staff, and it was an experience which was rewarding in so many ways.

Liam Kelley: The Trinity Yard School is unique both as an institution and an experience. I worked at TYS for over a year as a lead teacher with a group of truly amazing, dedicated, and incredibly hardworking individuals – both Ghanaian and American. My time at TYS was challenging at times, but ultimately left me with a much better understanding of the Ghanaian people and my own place in a world ripe with opportunity and diversity. The set of skills I gained have impacted almost every aspect of my life – personal, professional, and spiritual.

SpeedKingz/Shutterstock.com/ID/BR

2. Does any of them mention what kind of volunteering they really do? Write the answer in your notebook.

3. Look at the title of the text on the next page and answer the questions below in your notebook.

   a. Do you think the objective of the text is to introduce other people who do volunteering or to give some type of guidance?

   b. Who will be more interested in reading the text: people who already do volunteering or people who never did volunteering?

Exploring the text

1. Read the text on the next page about kinds of volunteering work and discuss it with a classmate.

Dictionary 7

volunteer *noun* UK /vɒl.ən'tɪər/ US /vɑː.lən'tɪr/

Definition: a person who does something, especially helping other people, willingly and without being forced or paid to do it.

Available at https://dictionary.cambridge.org/pt/dicionario/ingles/volunteer?q=volunteer+. Accessed on March 10, 2022.

YANCOM/ID/BR

Ideas to help you choose what kind of volunteering you should do

If you'd like to support a cause but can't afford to donate money, you can donate your time instead. Find what's right for you:

Help kids learn and grow. Become a camp counselor, or volunteer for an after-school sports program.

Play with pets at a local animal shelter. Most shelters depend on volunteers to keep the cats and dogs happy and well exercised.

Help the environment. Join a conservation group. Take part in a local park cleanup day. You don't have to be an outdoorsy type — if you can't picture yourself hauling trees up a hill, you could help out in a park office or education center.

Support a health-related cause. It can feel good to donate your time to an organization that offers help to people with an illness.

When you're calling an organization, it's best to ask for a volunteer coordinator. Most places will ask you to come for an interview, which is usually pretty casual. You might want to ask if you can observe some other volunteers in action to get a feel for the work before you commit.

Adapted from https://kidshealth.org/en/teens/volunteering.html. Accessed on March 10, 2022.

2. Based on the information in the text, what kind of volunteering would you recommend to these people? Answer in your notebook.

a. Diego is 22 years old. He is studying Veterinary Medicine in college. He has some free time during the week.

b. Pedro and Amanda are always promoting events at school. When they give parties they take care of all the details.

c. Kate's very friendly and she likes to talk in public. People always pay attention on what she says.

Post-reading

1. Do you know what "interdisciplinary work" is? It is a work that people do with resources from different areas. This means that people work together on the same project using resources from different fields. Look back at the text above and talk to your classmates about two abilities you would like to practice.

2. Think about a kind of volunteering that could be useful for your community. Then, think about a way people with the two abilities you selected above can work together for the same cause and talk about them to your classmates.

Rawpixel.com/Shutterstock.com/ID/BR

Não escreva no livro.

Grammar bits

Modal verbs

1. Read the following sentences.. Then, do the activities in the *Making sense* box.

A It teaches humbleness, something I **could** use.

B If you **can't** picture yourself hauling trees up a hill, you could help out in a park office.

C You **might** want to ask if you can observe some other volunteers in action.

D You don't **have to** be an outdoorsy type.

Making sense

Look at the examples above and pay attention to the verbs in **bold**. In your notebook, write the appropriate combination of numbers-letters.

a. The idea of **ability** is expressed in sentence I.

b. The idea of **obligation** is expressed in sentence II.

c. The idea of **possibility** is expressed in sentences III and IV.

Na sentença C, o verbo *might* pode ser substituído por *may*.

Claudio Chiyo/ID/BR

2. Write in your notebook at least five sentences about some people you know. Use the ideas from the two boxes, if you want. Look at the example.

My sister could tell stories for children in orphanages.

My sister... My mother... My father... My uncle... My aunt... My...	... can collect books for poor students. ... might help a lot in my community. ... could walk a neighbor's dog twice a week. ... could visit a home for senior citizens. ... can/could/might...

3. Suppose there is a project in your school for volunteer work. Work in groups, asking your colleagues what they could do to help. Follow the model.

Student A: How can you help? / How could you help?

Student B: I can/could/might...

Hobbit/Shutterstock.com/ID/BR

4. In your notebook, write three sentences for each topic. Follow the models.

I can... *They can...* *Students have to.../must...*

a. Abilities you have that are important to do volunteer work.

b. Abilities your friends have that are important to do volunteer work.

c. Rules for students at your school.

5. Read this excerpt of Nelson Mandela's autobiography. Then, use your imagination and speculate about what the people below said to Mandela. In your notebook, write the correct answer in each case.

Suns Design/Shutterstock.com/ID/BR

Macdonald Purnell/Arquivo da Editora

[...] The schoolhouse consisted of a single room, with a Western-style roof, on the other side of the hill from Qunu. I was seven years old, and on the day before I was to begin, my father took me aside and told me that I must be dressed properly for school. Until that time, I, like all the other boys in Qunu, had worn only a blanket, which was wrapped around one shoulder and pinned at the waist. My father took a pair of his trousers and cut them at the knee. He told me to put them on, which I did, and they were roughly the correct length, although the waist was far too large. My father then took a piece of string and cinched the trousers at the waist. I must have been a comical sight, but I have never owned a suit I was prouder to wear than my father's cut-off pants.

On the first day of school, my teacher, Miss Mdingane, gave each of us an English name and said that from thenceforth that was the name we would answer to in school. This was the custom among Africans in those days and was undoubtedly due to the British bias of our education. The education I received was a British education, in which British ideas, British culture, British institutions, were automatically assumed to be superior. There was no such thing as African culture. [...]

Nelson Mandela. *Long walk to freedom*: the autobiography of Nelson Mandela. Back Bay Books, 1994 (Part 1, The village of Qunu, p. 13-14).

a. Mandela's father said, "You **I** (**can't** / **can**) go to school wearing what you wear every day. You **II** (**have to** / **don't have to**) dress properly".

b. Mandela's father said, "Don't worry, son. I **III** (**can** / **can't**) make your school uniform".

c. Mandela's teacher said, "Kids, you **IV** (**can** / **can't**) use your African names in school".

d. Mandela's teacher said, "In this class you **V** (**must** / **don't have to**) study about the history of England".

Go to **Grammar reference** (unit 3).

Discussion point

- Em sua autobiografia, Nelson Mandela diz que sua professora só valorizava a cultura britânica durante as aulas. Por que você acha que isso acontecia?
- Você acha que a cultura brasileira deve ser valorizada nas matérias que você estuda na escola, especialmente nas aulas de inglês? Por quê?

Não escreva no livro.

Words, words, words

Qualities of a good volunteer

1. These short sentences summarize some recommendations on how to make the most of your volunteer work. In your notebook, write the appropriate combination of numbers-letters.

Dictionary 8

stir *verb* UK /stɜːr/ US /stɝː/

Definition: to wake up or begin to move or take action.

Available at https://dictionary.cambridge.org/dictionary/english/stir. Accessed on May 5, 2022.

I Be cooperative	IV Be enthusiastic	VII Be selfless
II Be organized	V Be well-trained	VIII Be open-minded
III Be reliable	VI Be friendly	IX Be respectful

A Being energetic and having a positive attitude can help to motivate yourself and others. Enthusiastic people always tend to stir those around them to positive action.

B You should be able to follow through on your commitment. All charity organisations rely on their volunteers to be successful. [...] A volunteer should be able to be on time and do their work so that they can produce the best results for the organisation.

C Volunteering involves many workers who are trying to reach the same goals you are. [...] You should be able to follow orders without complaining. If you show initiative you might also be able to grow your leadership skills.

D Since there is usually so much work to do, it is great to possess good organisational skills. Tasks become easier to complete and more manageable.

Adapted from https://annualmeeting.midwife.org/acnm-annual-meeting-student-volunteer-sign-up/. Accessed on March 10, 2022.

2. Read the recommendations above and choose the most meaningful piece of advice for you. Write it in your notebook.

3. Read the options of activity 1 again and match them to their opposites below. Write the combination of letters-numbers in your notebook.

A Be unreliable	E Be unfriendly
B Be narrow-minded	F Be uncooperative
C Be selfish	G Be badly-trained
D Be unenthusiastic	H Be disorganized

4. Talk to a classmate about volunteering using the adjectives of activity 1. Then, write some sentences in your notebook. Follow the example.

Volunteers can't be selfish. They must be selfless.

Open your ears

1. Can your friends count on you? In your notebook, write what would you do in the following situations using the words in the box.

Yes	No	It depends

a. If a friend calls me in the middle of the night to talk about a problem, I listen to him or her.

b. If a friend asks me for some money saying that she or he will pay me back only next month, I lend it.

c. If a friend asks me to wear my new pair of sneakers for the whole weekend, I lend it.

2. Talk to a classmate. Compare your answers in activity 1 and explain why you chose **yes, no** or **it depends.**

9 **3.** You are going to listen to a song about a person who can be a good friend. Close your book and listen to the recording. Try to write in your notebook the words that you listen during the song. Then, join a group and talk about what you could understand.

You've Got A Friend In Me

By Randy Newman

You've got a friend in me
You've got a friend in me
When the road looks rough ahead
And you're miles and miles
From your nice warm bed
You just remember what your old pal said
Boy, you've got a friend in me
Yeah, you've got a friend in me

You've got a friend in me
You've got a friend in me
You've got troubles, I've got 'em too
There isn't anything I wouldn't do for you
We stick together and we see it through
Cause you've got a friend in me
You've got a friend in me

Some other folks might be
A little bit smarter than I am
Bigger and stronger too Maybe
But none of them will ever love you
The way I do
It's me and you, boy

And as the years go by
Our friendship will never die
You're gonna see it's our destiny
You've got a friend in me
You've got a friend in me
You've got a friend in me

Available at https://www.azlyrics.com/lyrics/randynewman/youvegotafriendinme.html. Accessed on May 5, 2022. (Originally recorded by Randy Newman.)

Casablanka/Shutterstock.com/ID/BR

4. Open your book. Read the lyrics and check the words that you wrote.

5. Based on the lyrics above, discuss these questions:

a. Do you think this persona is sincere?

b. Is it always possible to be a great friend?

c. Do you think the singer is talking about a friend or a girlfriend? Why?

Não escreva no livro.

Speaker's corner

Presenting a speech in the classroom

1. Look at this picture and talk about what is going on.

Anderson Sanchez/ID/BR

2. Get ready to give a speech for your classmates about the importance of volunteering. Consider the following ideas:
   - what problems there are in your community;
   - what people can do to help;
   - what makes a good volunteer;
   - why volunteering is important for the community and for the person who helps.

3. Read these tips in order to give your speech with more confidence.
   - Research your topic. Take detailed notes.
   - Decide which information is necessary, and cut the rest.
   - Familiarize yourself with your topic and write your speech.
   - Ask your teacher to check your text. After that, write notes on index cards. Don't forget to use large and neat letters.
   - Practice your speech out loud until you are confident with it. Give your speech to things around your room. For example, a teddy bear, a doll, your cat, your dog...
   - Choose what visual aids you will use to help you.
   - When you have learned your presentation well, practice it in front of your family members or friends.
   - Go to school and give your speech with confidence!

   While you are presenting your speech:
   - Put your notes in a place where you can see them easily.
   - Pause after important points.
   - Pronounce your words clearly and vary the way you speak to avoid a "robot-like" presentation.
   - Don't read directly from your notes. Look at them sometimes to refresh your memory only.
   - Close your speech by thanking the audience. Ask if they have any questions about the topic.

Source: https://www.wikihow.com/Give-a-Speech-in-Front-of-Your-Class. Accessed on March 10, 2022.

Não escreva no livro.

Pen to paper

Completing an online form

Pre-writing

1. Look at these three texts. Who normally creates this type of text? Answer in your notebook.

Illustrations: Graphorama/ID/BR

Illustrations: Graphorama/ID/BR

Illustrations: Graphorama/ID/BR

2. What is the objective of the texts above? Write the answer in your notebook.

A To give hints on how to do volunteer work successfully.

B To encourage people to become volunteers.

C To explain the type of volunteer work people can do.

Follow these steps to complete a form to become a volunteer

1. Imagine you are interested in becoming a volunteer in some area. Think about how you could be helpful. Do you have any experience? If yes, what kind of work have you already done? Write a paragraph in English in your notebook describing your experience.

2. What are your abilities? List in your notebook a few things you know how to do well. For example: drawing cartoons; playing a musical instrument; cooking; knitting; etc.

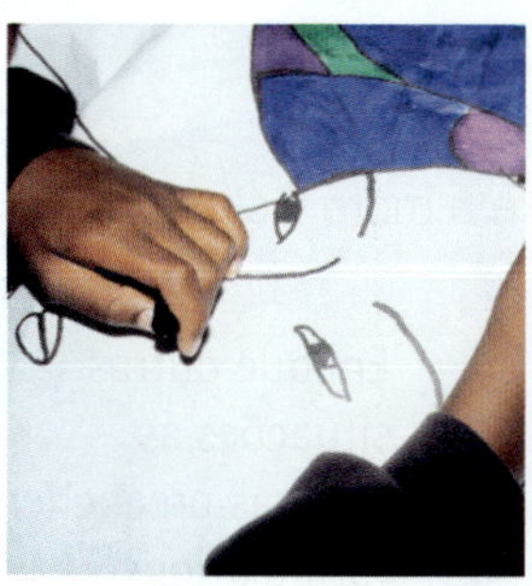
david sanger photography/Alamy/Fotoarena

Zirconicusso/Shutterstock.com/ID/BR

Michal Modzelewski/Shutterstock.com/ID/BR

Claude Beaubien/Shutterstock.com/ID/BR

3. Imagine that you saw on a website that an organization is seeking volunteers. Read the application form on the next page. Then, make a copy in your notebook and fill in your own data. In the *Experiences or Skills* field use the notes you took in the previous activity.

Não escreva no livro.

Please complete this application form and press the Submit Button when you have finished. One of our volunteer coordinators will contact you in 5 to 10 business days.

* Required Information

Date*	May 16, 2024	Age (only if under 18)	13
Name*	Olivia Smith		
Street Address*	987 Central Avenue		
City*	San Diego	State* CA	Zip Code* CA 12345
Daytime Phone*	(555) 555–5555	Alternate Phone	(555) 333–3333
Email*	oliviasmith@homebox1.com		
Occupation	Student		
Experiences or Skills	Reading Singing and playing the guitar Knitting Card playing Playing board games Watercolor painting		

Check your option in each item.

1 [ ] I prefer to work alone. [X] I prefer to work as part of a team.

2 [X] I prefer to serve children. [ ] I prefer to serve adults.

3 [ ] I prefer office/computer work. [ ] I prefer manual labor.

4 [ ] I am better behind the scenes (phone contact, for example). [X] I prefer to take a more visible role.

5 Causes that are important to me:

[ ] hunger [X] environment [ ] education

[X] animals [ ] health [ ] digital inclusion

Em que outras situações as pessoas preenchem formulários? Eles são sempre *on-line*?

Submit **Clear**

Focus on culture

Clown Doctors

Trust me, I'm a clown doctor: young Chinese patients are getting a taste of Western 'alternative medicine'

Dickson Lee/South China Morning Post/Getty Images

Wearing a round, red plastic nose, a colourful suit, and sometimes an outrageous wig, Song Longchao is affectionately referred to as "clown brother" by his young patients.

As a nurse at the children's surgery department of Sichuan Provincial People's Hospital in Chengdu, Song, 29, has spent much of his spare time in the past four years playing the fool in the hope of bringing joy and laughter to everyone on the wards.

Clown doctors appeared in the United States about four decades ago, and the idea spread to other Western countries. The phenomenon became the subject of the 1998 Hollywood film *Patch Adams*, starring Robin Williams.

But China, it is a new phenomenon, and few people know of the practice, which is based on the theory that humour can complement medical treatment.

Song said he discovered clowning in 2015, when senior doctor colleagues returned with the idea after studying in overseas hospitals and asked staff if they were interested in it.

"I said I would try because I love doing volunteer work, and clown doctoring seems able to help patients," he said.

Four years later, the hospital has a 100-strong clown team – all volunteers and all doctors or nurses.

"After these years performing as a clown, I found it makes people happy and it makes me happy, too," said Song. "It's truly meaningful."

Available at https://www.scmp.com/news/china/society/article/3024057/trust-me-im-clown-doctor-young-chinese-patients-are-getting. Accessed on March 15, 2022.

1. Read the text and talk with your colleagues about the following questions.

a. What do clown doctors usually do?

b. What do you think is the difference between the work of a "normal" doctor and the work of a clown doctor?

2. Do you know anyone who works as a clown doctor? Do you have clown doctors working in your town? Do some research to find out if there are any groups or organizations of this kind in your town or in your state. Create a poster with the material you have researched.

Self-assessment

Reflect about your own learning

assessment | learning | reflect | autonomy | English | responsibility | feedback

Freepik/ID/BR

I do it with confidence.	I do it well.	I can get better.

1. Como você avalia o seu aprendizado nesta unidade? Reflita.

a. Que parte da unidade (seção, texto, imagem, mensagem do tutor, etc.) mais lhe agradou? Por quê?

b. Qual foi a parte de que você menos gostou? Por quê?

c. Você se lembra de alguma coisa que viu nesta unidade e que o ajudou fora da aula de inglês?

2. O que você pode fazer para melhorar seu aprendizado de inglês? Observe as opções abaixo e pense a respeito delas.

- Ler mais.
- Fazer mais atividades.
- Solucionar dúvidas com o professor.
- Trocar ideias com os colegas.
- Ouvir músicas em inglês.
- Assistir a filmes em inglês com legendas.

imtmphoto/Shutterstock.com/ID/BR

UNIT 4 Health

In this unit you will be dealing with different situations related to health. The main text focuses on healthy eating habit. All over the unit you will be engaged in different activities that feature the following elements:

- **Genres:** poster; recipe
- **Vocabulary:** types of food
- **Grammar:** countable and uncountable nouns

Quick challenge

Read the questions below. Scan the pages of this unit and write the answers in your notebook.

a. What section shows the picture of a carrot cake?

b. What section shows a recipe of a salad?

c. One of these pictures is not used in this unit. Which one?

1

Boris Horvat/AFP

3

Claudio Chiyo/ID/BR

2

Bogdan Ionescu/Shutterstock.com/ID/BR

4

Brent Hofacker/Shutterstock.com/ID/BR

Não escreva no livro.

A first approach

Talking about the topic

1. What types of texts are these? What do they have in common?
2. What is the subject of each of these texts?
3. How important do you think this type of message is?
4. Do you think these messages would have the same impact without the pictures? Why (not)?

1

Arquivo/© The State of Queensland (Queensland Health)

2

Arquivo/Healthy Kids

3

Arquivo/© The State of Queensland (Queensland Health)

4

Arquivo/Courtesy of the U.S. Department of State

Não escreva no livro.

5

Arquivo/© The State of Queensland (Queensland Health)

6

Arquivo/Centers for Disease Control and Prevention

Exploring the topic

Dictionary 10

suitable *adjective* UK /ˈsuː.tə.bəl/ /ˈsjuː.tə.bəl/ US /ˈsuː.t̬ə.bəl/

Definition: acceptable or right for someone or something.

Available at https://dictionary.cambridge.org/dictionary/english/suitable. Accessed on March 15, 2022.

1. Four of the sentences below **do not** refer to the topics presented in the posters. Which are they? Write them in your notebook.

a. Hygienic habits are important to prevent health problems.

b. In case you wake up thirsty in the middle of night, keep a glass of drinking water close to your bed.

c. Immunization campaigns help protect people from some infectious diseases.

d. When you wash your hair, remember to use a suitable shampoo.

e. It is important to include in our diet healthy items like apple, banana, watermelon, zucchini, potato, and carrot.

f. Don't take medicine without a medical prescription.

g. It is very important to brush your teeth after meals and before going to bed.

2. Practice your ability to work with non-verbal language. In a sheet of paper, add images to create a poster for a campaign. Then, share it with your classmates.

Looking around

1. What kind of health campaigns are there where you live?

2. In your opinion, are these campaigns successful in producing the desired or intended result? Why (not)?

3. What kind of media do you think can be more effective to promote this type of message?

4. Do you think these campaigns can change people's behaviors and attitudes?

Não escreva no livro.

Reading corner

Pre-reading

1. Read these opinions about food and healthy eating habits. Then, in pairs, study each case and form your own opinion about it: Is it a myth or a fact?

   I As long as I skip a meal, I can eat whatever I want at the next one.

   II As long as a food package says "all natural" on it, it's healthy to eat.

   III If I'm not overweight, I don't have to be careful about what I eat.

   IV A fast-food cheeseburger is a balanced meal, because it has meat, cheese, bread, and vegetables.

   V Sugar gives you energy. If you need a boost mid-afternoon or before playing sports, eat a candy bar.

Adapted from http://www.sharonzarabi.com/documents/Food%20Smarts%20Myths%20&%20Facts.pdf. Accessed on March 15, 2022.

Exploring the text

1. Read these paragraphs. They contradict the common beliefs above. Match each sentence in the previous activity to its corresponding paragraph below. Write the combinations of numbers-letters in your notebook.

A Even if something is labeled "all natural", it can still contain tons of sugar, saturated fats, or other things that can be bad for you. Some snacks labeled "all natural" can contain just as much fat as a candy bar! It's important to read the Nutrition Facts label and the ingredients list.

B Fast-food cheeseburgers, and almost everything else served at fast-food restaurants, are very high in fats, calories, and sodium. It is okay to enjoy these foods once in a while, but if you're eating them a couple of times a week or more, this is too much, and you might want to try making healthier choices.

C Even if you've never had a problem with your weight, it's important to choose healthy foods every day. If you think of your body as a machine, then you'll want to use the very best fuel to keep that machine going strong, and that means staying away from junk food. Also, if you develop poor eating habits now, you may have a lot of problems with your weight and health in the years to come.

D It's never a good idea to skip a meal, and it won't make up for eating unhealthy foods, or eating too much, the next time you eat. It's important to eat three normal-sized and healthy meals a day, and even a few snacks in between, so your body has energy when it needs it.

E "Simple" sugars like those found in chocolate, cookies, candies, and cakes definitely cause spikes in your blood sugar level, which may make you feel a quick shot of energy in your system. But after that first rush, blood sugar drops sharply, and you'll suddenly feel like you have less energy than when you started!

Adapted from http://www.sharonzarabi.com/documents/Food%20Smarts%20Myths%20&%20Facts.pdf. Accessed on March 15, 2022.

2. Read the title and the introductory paragraph below. They are of the text on the previous page. In your notebook, write the appropriate combinations of letters-numbers.

> ### Food smarts: myths and facts
>
> When it comes to food and eating healthy, you probably hear a lot of opinions and "facts" from your parents, friends, relatives, and teachers. This is partly because older people may have grown up when there was different food information out there, and partly because food companies and advertising want you to believe certain things in order to get you to buy their products. [...]
>
> Available at http://www.sharonzarabi.com/documents/Food%20Smarts%20Myths%20&%20Facts.pdf. Accessed on March 15, 2022.

Kanate/Shutterstock.com/ID/BR

a. O título do texto já indica ao leitor que há um histórico de que existem...

- **I** poucas verdades sobre o assunto a ser tratado.
- **II** apenas lendas sobre o assunto a ser tratado.
- **III** lendas e verdades sobre o assunto a ser tratado.

b. O autor espera que seu texto seja lido especialmente por...

- **I** pais e mães.
- **II** leitores jovens.
- **III** professores.
- **IV** nutricionistas.

3. Por que o autor preferiu colocar a palavra *facts* entre aspas no texto? Escolha uma das alternativas abaixo ou pense em outra possibilidade. Answer in your notebook.

a. Para indicar que essa fala não é dele, mas de outras pessoas.

b. Para reforçar que esses fatos são reais e não mitos.

c. Para mostrar que esses fatos não são reais.

4. Look at the definitions below. Then, look at the highlighted words in activity 1. Match them to create a short glossary and write the combinations in your notebook.

- **I** incapable of absorbing or dissolving more of something
- **II** falls
- **III** food that is bad for your health
- **IV** material, such as gasoline, that makes a machine work
- **V** small meals, eaten in a hurry
- **VI** sometimes; not often
- **VII** table or sticker with information about a product
- **VIII** two or more times

Claudio Chiyo/ID/BR

Quando há palavras desconhecidas em um texto, às vezes precisamos recorrer ao próprio texto para entendê-las. Pense: "O que esta palavra quer dizer neste contexto?". Levante hipóteses e tente substituir a palavra desconhecida pelo significado provável. Releia a sentença e se pergunte: "Isso faz sentido?".

Não escreva no livro.

Words, words, words

Types of food

New Africa/Shutterstock.com/ID/BR

1. Substitute the symbols ✪, ✹, ❒, ❖, and ◎ by vowels and write the words in your notebook. The first one is done for you.

a. L ✹ TT ◎ C ✹ = LETTUCE
   ✪ R ◎ G ◎ L ✪
   S P ❒ N ✪ C H
   C ✪ B B ✪ G ✹

b. B ✪ N ✪ N ✪
   ❖ R ✪ N G ✹
   P ❒ N ✹ ✪ P P L ✹
   P ✪ P ✪ Y ✪
   G R ✪ P ✹
   ✪ P P L ✹
   W ✪ T ✹ R M ✹ L ❖ N

c. P ❖ T ✪ T ❖
   T ❖ M ✪ T ❖
   C ✪ R R ❖ T
   C ❖ R N
   Z ◎ C C H ❒ N ❒
   C ◎ C ◎ M B ✹ R

d. M ❒ L K
   Y ❖ G ◎ R T
   C H ✹ ✹ S ✹
   B ◎ T T ✹ R

e. B R ✹ ✪ D
   R ❒ C ✹
   B ✹ ✪ N S
   C ✹ R ✹ ✪ L S
   P ✪ S T ✪
   F L ❖ ◎ R

f. C H ❒ C K ✹ N
   B ✹ ✹ F
   F ❒ S H
   ✹ G G S
   P ❖ R K

g. ❒ C ✹ C R ✹ ✪ M
   C ✪ K ✹
   P ❒ ✹
   B ◎ B B L ✹ G ◎ M
   F R ❒ ✹ S
   C H ❖ C ❖ L ✪ T ✹
   S ❖ D ✪

Claudio Chiyo/ID/BR

O modo como os britânicos (ingleses, escoceses, irlandeses e galeses) pronunciam *tomato* e *potato* é diferente da maneira como os estadunidenses o fazem. Os britânicos pronunciam algo como "to-maa-tow" e "po-taa-tow". Já os estadunidenses pronunciam algo como "to-may-tow" e "po-tay-tow". O idioma é o mesmo, porém com variantes.

picturepartners/Shutterstock.com/ID/BR

Tom Grundy/Alamy/Fotoarena

2. In your notebook, organize the words from the criptogram into a chart, using the categories below. If you want, add more items to each category.

I grains

Khudoliy/Shutterstock.com/ID/BR

II fruits

Viktor1/Shutterstock.com/ID/BR

III vegetables

Ana Blazic Pavlovic/Shutterstock.com/ID/BR

IV dairy products

margouillat photo/Shutterstock.com/ID/BR

V greens

Eising Studio/StockFood/Latinstock

VI meat and eggs

New Africa/Shutterstock.com/ID/BR

VII fats, oils and sweets

Aparecida de Sousa/Acervo da fotógrafa

3. Look at this shopping list and do these activities in your notebook.

a. The person probably wants to make...

I a lasagna.

II a carrot cake.

III an apple pie.

b. Match the containers and measures with the ingredients. Some ingredients may correspond to more than one container or measure.

YANCOM/ID/BR

I a liter	**III** a kilo	**V** a dozen	**VII** a can
II a box	**IV** a bottle	**VI** a bunch	**VIII** a carton

Milk.

Doomu/Shutterstock.com/ID/BR

Baking soda.

Naviya/Shutterstock.com/ID/BR

Eggs.

Sea Wave/Shutterstock.com/ID/BR

Flour.

Timmary/Shutterstock.com/ID/BR

Cocoa powder.

Mama_mia/Shutterstock.com/ID/BR

Carrots.

5 Second Studio/Shutterstock.com/ID/BR

Sugar.

Koosen/Shutterstock.com/ID/BR

Oil.

Bogdan Ionescu/Shutterstock.com/ID/BR

Não escreva no livro.

Grammar bits

Countable and uncountable nouns

1. Read the list of ingredients of a Brazilian-style carrot cake. Write in your notebook **C** (countable) or **U** (uncountable) for each ingredient below.

a. eggs
b. honey
c. milk
d. carrots
e. flour
f. vegetable oil

Brazilian-style carrot cake with chocolate sauce

Serves: 10

Paulo Vilela/Shutterstock.com/ID/BR

Ingredients

2 cups white sugar
3 eggs
½ cup vegetable oil
3 carrots, quartered
2 cups all-purpose flour
1 tablespoon baking powder

Chocolate sauce

½ cup white sugar
½ cup cocoa powder
6 tablespoons milk
2 tablespoons unsalted butter

Available at https://www.allrecipes.com/recipe/254749/brazilian-style-carrot-cake-with-chocolate-sauce/. Accessed on March 15, 2022.

2. Read the ingredients again and, in your notebook, answer these questions.

a. How many carrots do you need to prepare this recipe?
b. How much all-purpose flour do you need to make this carrot cake?
c. How many tablespoons of unsalted butter do you need?
d. How many eggs do you need if you want to prepare two cakes?
e. How many people can you serve with this recipe?

Dictionary 11

caster sugar *noun* [U] UK /'kɑː.stə ʃʊg.ər/
US /'kæs.tɚ ʃʊg.ɚ/
Definition: white sugar with very small grains, often used in cooking.

Available at https://dictionary.cambridge.org/pt/dicionario/ingles/caster-sugar. Accessed on March 15, 2022.

3. In your notebook, complete the sentences using **many** or **much**.

a. There isn't **I** milk in the fridge.
b. Carla has **II** friends. She's going to invite them for dinner.
c. I put too **III** caster sugar on my donut.
d. How **IV** water do you drink every day?

Making sense

Read the sentences below and complete them in your notebook.

a. We use *how many* and *many* to talk about...

I countable and singular nouns.

II uncountable and plural nouns.

III countable and plural nouns.

b. We use *how much* and *much* to talk about...

I countable and singular nouns.

II uncountable and singular nouns.

III uncountable and plural nouns.

4. Match the following questions to their appropriate answers. Then, write the combinations of numbers–letters in your notebook.

I Do we use any water to prepare a carrot cake with chocolate icing?

II Would you like some cake, Melissa?

III Do you need any help to prepare the cake?

IV Do I need to buy any oranges for this recipe?

A Yes, please. I'd love some.

B No, you don't. You just need to buy some carrots.

C No, we don't use any. We use some oil and milk.

D Yes, I need some, please.

Making sense

Read the sentences below and complete them in your notebook.

a. We use *some* in A sentences.

I affirmative

II negative

b. We use *any* in B sentences and in questions.

I affirmative

II negative

c. We use *some* in questions when we expect the answer C.

I "yes"

II "no"

Você sabia que, em inglês, o substantivo *music* é incontável? Quando alguém diz *I like music*, significa que a pessoa gosta de música em geral. Quando queremos falar se gostamos ou não de um tipo específico de música, usamos a palavra *song*, por exemplo, *I don't like romantic songs.* ou *These are my favorite songs.*

Claudio Chiyo/ID/BR

Não escreva no livro.

Open your ears

1. Helsinki is located in Finland and it's well-known for being a cold city. What do you think the children eat at school there? Write the names in your notebook.

A

Robert Stedman Pte Ltd/Shutterstock.com/ID/BR

Cheese.

D

Neil langan/Shutterstock.com/ID/BR

Crisps.

G

Tawatchai Prontip/Shutterstock.com/ID/BR

Rice.

B

Lukas Gojda/Shutterstock.com/ID/BR

Hamburger.

E

Smelenna/Shutterstock.com/ID/BR

Crispbread.

H

Nitr/Shutterstock.com/ID/BR

Salad.

C

MemoryMan/Shutterstock.com/ID/BR

Pork curry.

F

Baibaz/Shutterstock.com/ID/BR

Chocolate.

I

Kabachki.photo/Shutterstock.com/ID/BR

Milk.

12 2. Now, you are going to listen to someone explaining what children eat at school in Helsinki. Check your answers and share your impressions with a classmate.

12 3. Listen to the audio again and answer the questions in your notebook.

a. What does the person say about school lunches?

I They are free and compulsory.

II They are free and children can choose what to eat.

III Children must pay for their lunches.

b. What does the boy choose?

I He chooses chips.

II He chooses salad.

A culinária finlandesa utiliza ingredientes naturais e frescos. Entre seus pratos tradicionais está o Poronkäristys, mistura de carne de rena, purê de batatas com um molho de frutas vermelhas. Você conhece culinárias de outros países? Quais são os pratos tradicionais de cada uma?

Claudio Chiyo/ID/BR

Não escreva no livro.

Speaker's corner

Making a simple recipe

1. You and your friend are at the kitchen on a Sunday afternoon. You are both hungry. Your friend has found on the Internet an easily made recipe. Read the recipe below.

YANCOM/ID/BR

Waldorf salad with yogurt

Charlotte Lake/Shutterstock.com/ID/BR

Ingredients

Serves: 4

3 tart apples – peeled, cored and chopped

1 tablespoon lemon juice

1 cup seedless grapes

2 stalks celery, chopped

2 green onions, chopped

2 tablespoons mayonnaise

2 tablespoons plain yogurt

3 tablespoons apple juice

1/4 teaspoon celery seed

1 bunch watercress, trimmed and chopped

2 tablespoons chopped walnuts

Method

Prep: 20 min

- In a large bowl, combine the apples and lemon juice.
- Add the grapes, celery and green onion; toss.
- In a small bowl, whisk together the mayonnaise, the yogurt, the apple juice and celery seeds.
- Spoon over the apple mixture, and toss gently.
- Wash the watercress, and dry thoroughly.
- Arrange greens on individual salad plates.
- Mound the apple mixture on top, and sprinkle with the walnuts.

Available at https://www.allrecipes.com/recipe/14414/waldorf-salad-with-yogurt/. Accessed on March 15, 2022.

2. You and your friend decide to make this recipe. He or she will be at the computer and you will be responsible for preparing the recipe. What questions can you ask your friend during the preparation? Write them in your notebook.

a. How many green onions do we need?

b. How much is it?

c. We only have one apple. Is that OK?

d. Can we use pineapple instead of apple?

e. Is there a drugstore near here?

f. What kind of nut do we need?

g. What's your favorite food?

h. Do we need any yogurt?

i. How many servings does it make?

j. Are you a good doctor?

3. What other questions can you ask your friend in case you have doubts during the preparation of the recipe? Write them in your notebook.

4. Let's prepare the recipe. Work in pairs (Student A and Student B). Student A reads the recipe and Student B answers and asks questions whenever necessary.

Pen to paper

Designing a poster for a healthier lifestyle

Pre-writing

1. Look back at the different posters in this unit. Observe how they are designed. Write in your notebook the common elements in most of them.

a. An interesting sentence to get the reader's attention.

b. Use of short sentences.

c. Long paragraphs with detailed explanations.

d. Creative images to illustrate the topic and attract more viewers.

e. Questions to make the reader think.

f. Lots of numbers and statistics about the topic.

g. Logotype of the company or organization behind the campaign.

h. Effective use of colors and fonts.

Arquivo/© The State of Queensland (Queensland Health)

Arquivo/© The State of Queensland (Queensland Health)

Arquivo/© The State of Queensland (Queensland Health)

Arquivo/Centers for Disease Control and Prevention

Arquivo/Healthy Kids

Arquivo/Courtesy of the U.S. Department of State

Um bom pôster deve informar rapidamente aquilo que o público necessita saber. Não precisa ter muitas imagens, mas a que for escolhida deve prender a atenção do leitor. A escolha das cores é importante. Uma cor inadequada pode prejudicar a campanha.

Claudio Chiyo/ID/BR

Follow these steps to create a poster for a healthier lifestyle

1. Choose a topic about healthy life style that interests you. Decide on a message what you want to communicate. Do some research to make sure the information you include is accurate. Make a draft of your poster in your notebook. Choose the image(s) you want to use.

2. When you are happy with what you have, show your plan to your teacher or to a classmate. Ask them what they think. Based on your teacher's or classmate's feedback, make the necessary adjustments to your plan.

3. Now you are ready to produce your poster! Make it beautiful and effective!

Focus on culture

Eating smart

1. Do you think what we eat can influence our health? Discuss it with your classmates.

2. Read the text below with attention and copy into your notebook the words that you don't understand. Then, read the text again and try to find out their meaning.

The 6 Worst Foods for Your Brain

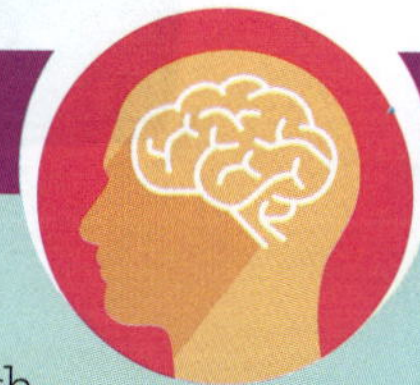

DrAfter123/iStock/Getty Images

1 Sugary Drinks

A high intake of sugary drinks may increase the risk of dementia. High fructose corn syrup (HFCS) may be especially harmful, causing brain inflammation and impairing memory and learning. Further studies in humans are needed.

2 Refined Carbs

A high intake of refined carbs with a high glycemic index (GI) and glycemic load (GL) may impair memory and intelligence, as well as increase the risk of dementia. These include sugars and highly processed grains like white flour.

3 Foods High in Trans Fats

Trans fats may be associated with impaired memory and the risk of Alzheimer's, but the evidence is mixed. Cutting out trans fats completely and increasing the unsaturated fats in your diet may be a good strategy.

4 Highly Processed Foods

Processed foods contribute to excess fat around the organs, which is associated with a decline in brain tissue. Additionally, Western-style diets may increase brain inflammation and impair memory, learning, brain plasticity and the blood-brain barrier.

5 Aspartame

Aspartame is an artificial sweetener found in many soft drinks and sugar-free products. It has been linked to behavioral and cognitive problems, though overall it is considered a safe product.

6 Fish High in Mercury

Mercury is a neurotoxic element that can be particularly harmful to developing fetuses and young children. The primary source in the diet is large predatory fish such as shark and swordfish. It is best to limit your intake of fish that are high in mercury.

Adapted from https://www.healthline.com/nutrition/worst-foods-for-your-brain. Accessed on March 15, 2022.

3. Look at the posters on the previous page again. How can we relate them to the topics in the text? Talk to your classmates about it.

4. In groups, choose a topic from the text, do some research to exemplify it, and create a poster using images and short sentences. Then, show it to your teacher and classmates.

Self-assessment

Reflect about your own learning

assessment · learning · reflect · autonomy · English · responsibility · feedback

Freepik/ID/BR

I do it with confidence.	I do it well.	I can get better.

1. Como você avalia seu aprendizado nesta unidade? Reflita.

a. Que parte da unidade (seção, texto, imagem, mensagem do tutor, etc.) mais lhe agradou? Por quê?

b. Qual foi a parte de que você menos gostou? Por quê?

c. Você se lembra de alguma coisa que viu nesta unidade e que o ajudou fora da aula de inglês?

2. O que você pode fazer para melhorar seu aprendizado de inglês? Observe as opções abaixo e pense a respeito delas.

- Ler mais.
- Fazer mais atividades.
- Solucionar dúvidas com o professor.
- Trocar ideias com os colegas.
- Ouvir músicas em inglês.
- Assistir a filmes em inglês com legendas.

Andresr/iStock/Getty Images

Não escreva no livro.

UNIT

5 Technology

In this unit you will have the opportunity to talk about something that is part of everything we do every day: technology. The main text will help you think about the pros and cons of a machine that most people have nowadays: a cell phone. All over this unit you will be engaged in activities that feature the following elements:

- **Genres:** guide; report
- **Vocabulary:** phrasal verbs
- **Grammar:** *there to be* (present & past); *used to*

Quick challenge

Read the questions below. Find the answers and write them in your notebook.

a. What are the names of the characters in the poster on page 71?

b. Where is a black and white photo in this unit?

c. What does the illustration in the *Open your ears* section show?

d. One of these pictures is not used in this unit. Which one?

1

George Tutumi/ID/BR

3

Maxx-Studio/Shutterstock.com/ID/BR

2

Zap Art/Getty Images

4

Nmedia/Shutterstock.com/ID/BR

Não escreva no livro.

A first approach

Talking about the topic

1

Georgejmclittle/Shutterstock.com/ID/BR

4

Kayla Dean/Alamy/Fotoarena

2

Radu Bercan/Shutterstock.com/ID/BR

5

Helder Almeida/Shutterstock.com/ID/BR

3

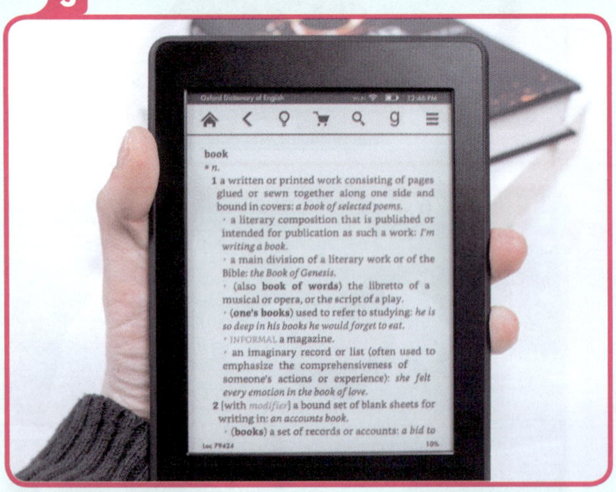

A. Aleksandravicius/Shutterstock.com/ID/BR

6

CandyrailN/Shutterstock.com/ID/BR

Não escreva no livro.

1. Are you familiar with all the types of technology represented on the previous page? What are they used for?

2. Which objects represented on the previous page are essential for most people nowadays and which are not? Why?

3. Can the use of electronic equipment have negative consequences? If so, which ones?

4. Do the advertising campaigns for those products mention the possible "bad side" of overusing electronic equipment?

Exploring the topic

1. Answer these questions in your notebook creating a chart similar to the example below. Pay attention to the structure of the question ("How many [*objects*] are there in [*a place*]?") to formulate the structure of the answer. The first one is done as a model.

How many...	your answers	your classmate's answers
... desktop computers are there in your house?	There are three desktop computers in my house.	

a. ... CD/DVD players are there in your house?
b. ... TV sets are there in your house?
c. ... cell phones are there in your house?
d. ... laptop computers are there in your house?
e. ... digital cameras are there in your house?
f. ... tablets are there in your house?
g. ... video game consoles are there in your house?

2. Use the questions above to interview a classmate. Write his or her answers in the "your classmate's answers" column in your notebook.

3. Now, in pairs, compare your answers to your classmate's. Are they similar? How can you explain the similarities or differences?

Looking around

1. Are all these technologies available in Brazil? Does everybody have access to them in your region?

2. In your opinion, how different were people's lives before the development of these technologies?

Estas atividades abrem uma boa oportunidade para rever conteúdos. Por exemplo, você se lembra de como usamos *there is* e *there are*? E *more ... than*?

Claudio Chiyo/ID/BR

Não escreva no livro.

Reading corner

Pre-reading

1. Talk about these questions with one or two classmates.

   a. Do you have a cell phone? What do you use it for?

   b. Does it have any features that you don't use? If so, why not?

   c. Are there situations in which people use cell phones inappropriately? If so, what are they?

2. These pictures are going to be used by a graphic designer in the creation of a poster. Help the graphic designer find where to put them on the next page. Write in your notebook the appropriate letter-number combination.

Illustrations: George Tutumi/ID/BR

GUIDE TO CELL PHONE ETIQUETTE

DOOFUS & Dashing

I Doofus talks loudly, so everyone will know how important he is.

Doofus sets his ringtone to "Let's Get It Started" so he can start a party wherever he goes.

Doofus texts others while meeting with friends, so he can keep his options open.

II Doofus turns his ringer volume up during movies, so he won't miss any important calls.

Doofus likes having intimate conversations in public places.

Doofus texts while driving, because he hears talking on cell phone at the steering wheel can cause accidents.

III Doofus never hangs up when ordering, because his friends are more important than coffee.

Dashing keeps his voice down when talking on his cell.

IV Dashing sets his phone on vibrate, so no one will hear it ring.

V Dashing turns off his cell phone when he's with others.

VI Dashing turns his cell phone off at the movies.

Dashing saves personal conversations for when he's alone.

VII Dashing pulls to the side of the road to take a call.

Dashing hangs up before getting in line.

Illustrations: George Tutumi/ID/BR

Adapted from https://bitrebels.com/geek/cell-phone-etiquette-don%e2%80%99t-be-a-jerk-infographic/. Accessed on March 10, 2022.

Não escreva no livro.

Exploring the text

1. Observe the text on the previous page and read the statements below. In your notebook, write the statements which you think are correct.
   a. It is a very formal guide.
   b. It is a very informal guide.
   c. The author uses the Simple present in the text.
   d. The author uses the Imperative in the text.
   e. The pictures are fine, but they are not essential for the understanding of the text.
   f. The sentences are fine, but they are not essential for the understanding of the text. The pictures are self-explanatory.
   g. The guide contains pieces of information that are relevant only for teenagers.
   h. The guide contains pieces of information that are relevant for cell phone users of all ages.

Dictionary 13

self-explanatory *adjective*
UK /ˌself.ɪk'splæn.ə.tri/ US /ˌself.ɪk'splæn.ə.-tɔːr.i/

Definition: easily understood from the information already given and not needing further explanation.

Available at http://dictionary.cambridge.org/dictionary/british/self-explanatory. Accessed on March 10, 2022.

2. Read these sentences. Decide if these opinions refer to Doofus's or to Dashing's personality. In your notebook, write **Do** for Doofus, **Da** for Dashing, or **?** if you are in doubt.
   a. He is a selfish and conceited person.
   b. He is a respectful and considerate person.
   c. He thinks he is more important than other people.
   d. He doesn't care about other people.
   e. He knows there are limits to his rights.
   f. He knows his responsibilities as a citizen.

3. Compare your answers in activity 2 to a classmate's. Then discuss these questions with him or her.
   a. Do you think it is fair to call one of the characters Doofus (= a foolish person)?
   b. Who do you identify yourself with: Doofus or Dashing? Explain.

4. Use your notebook to write which of Doofus' attitudes can irritate other people. Explain your answer.

5. Which of Doofus' attitudes can put other people's lives in danger? Why? Write the answers in your notebook.

Post-reading

1. Think of one more possible situation to add to the poster on the previous page. Create the pictures and the texts for Doofus and Dashing. Use your notebook.

Words, words, words

Phrasal verbs

Dictionary 14

gizmo *noun* UK /ˈɡɪz.məʊ/ US /ˈɡɪz.moʊ/

Definition: any small device with a particular purpose.

Available at https://dictionary.cambridge.org/dictionary/english/gizmo. Accessed on May 3, 2022.

1. Would you like to have a futuristic house? Talk to a classmate. Then read the texts below.

According to the website gizmodo.com, it is simple to **turn** your house **into** a futuristic place. You can simplify your life with home automation solutions. You can have a computer that **wakes** you **up**, **kicks** you **out** of bed, and makes your breakfast. How is it possible? **Find out** how in the text below.

X10 is a simple protocol that allows devices to communicate over electrical lines – that means it lets a computer tell your appliances to **turn on** and **off**. You can buy X10 kits for a few hundred dollars, and control all of your home gizmos via the web – so you could create a program that **turns on** your coffee pot and starts microwaving your oatmeal ten minutes after your alarm **goes off** and the actuators under your bed **push** you **up** into a sitting position.

mmaxer/Shutterstock.com/ID/BR

Available at https://gizmodo.com/10-ways-to-turn-your-house-into-a-futuristic-fortress-5772029. Accessed on March 10, 2022.

What is a smart house? What is domotics?

Smart home technology, also often referred to as home automation or domotics (from the Latin "domus" meaning home), provides homeowners security, comfort, convenience and energy efficiency by allowing them to control smart devices, often by a smart home app on their smartphone or other networked device.

Available at https://internetofthingsagenda.techtarget.com/definition/smart-home-or-building. Accessed on March 10, 2022.

2. Look at these phrasal verbs and find them in the texts above. Can you figure out the meaning of these phrasal verbs? Study the context and match them to the definitions below. Use your notebook.

A to find out	C to go off	E to kick out	G to push up
B to turn into	D to turn off	F to turn on	H to wake up

- I to learn by study, observation, or search
- II to start ringing, to make a characteristic sound
- III to eject forcefully
- IV to use force to move something into a different position
- V to become
- VI to cause to stop operating
- VII to cause to activate or operate
- VIII to cause to stop sleeping

Claudio Chiyo/ID/BR

O que será que *gizmo* significa, de acordo com o contexto? E o que você imagina que sejam os X10 *kits*? Acesse o *link* da Gizmodo para saber. Aproveite e pesquise mais sobre o X10: Quem o desenvolveu? Quando? Onde?

Não escreva no livro.

Speaker's corner

Giving instructions on how to use something

1. Look at this picture and talk about the questions.

a. What do you think the question marks near the man's head mean?

b. What is the man probably saying to the boy?

c. Is this kind of situation common or not?

Suryara Bernardi/ID/BR

2. Read each group of sentences. Who is saying these things? Write in your notebook the combination of letters-numbers.

A Somebody who doesn't know how to do something.

B Somebody who knows how to do something.

I Do you need any help? • Let me take a look. Maybe I can help you. • I see that you need some help. Can I do anything for you?

II I was wondering if you could help me install this computer. • Sorry to bother you, but could you help me install this computer? • Hey, can you help me install this computer?

III Sure, why not? • Oh, yes, of course. • Well, let me see what I can do for you.

3. Work in pairs. Prepare a conversation to act out to your class. Look at the context below. Then follow the steps.

Student A: You have just bought a new piece of electronic equipment.

Student B: You know how to use this equipment very well.

Step 1: Choose a piece of electronic equipment.

Science Photo/Shutterstock.com/ID/BR

Step 2: Think about common doubts a user may have. In your notebook, write down questions you would ask to clear up these doubts.

Step 3: Think about how to answer these questions. If necessary, check sites or manuals of the product in English.

Roman Arbuzov/Shutterstock.com/ID/BR

Step 4: Write down in your notebook the answers to the questions.

Framesira/Shutterstock.com/ID/BR

Step 5: Practice before the presentation. You may use the sentences you learned in activity 2 and the vocabulary studied in *Words, words, words*.

Não escreva no livro.

Grammar bits

There to be (present & past)

1. Look at these photos. Where are these people? What do they do? Complete the sentences using the words below. Use your notebook to write the answers.

A there is	**C** there weren't	**E** there were
B there are	**D** there was	**F** there wasn't

Arquivo/Agência O Globo

Marcos Tristão/Agência O Globo

1950's — Today

a. Nowadays, **I** men and women doing the same jobs in these places.
In the 50's, **II** basically only men in these places.

b. Nowadays, **III** cell phones and wireless phones in these places.
In the 50's, **IV** only landline telephones in these places.

c. Nowadays, **V** lots of computers in these places.
In the 50's, **VI** computers in these places. **VII** a lot of typewriters.

d. Nowadays, **VIII** access to the Internet in these places.
In the 50's, **IX** access to Internet in these places.

cell phone

Zeynep Demir/Shutterstock.com/ID/BR

wireless phone

2ban/iStock/Getty Images

landline phone

Maxx-Studio/Shutterstock.com/ID/BR

typewriter

Just2shutter/Shutterstock.com/ID/BR

Making sense

1. Do you still remember? Copy the correct option in your notebook.

In the present,

a. we use **there is** followed by nouns in the **I** (**singular / plural**).

b. we use **there are** followed by nouns in the **II** (**singular / plural**).

2. What do you notice in activity 1 above?

In the past,

a. we use **there was** followed by nouns in the **III** (**singular / plural**).

b. we use **there were** followed by nouns in the **IV** (**singular / plural**).

Não escreva no livro.

2. In your notebook, rewrite these sentences. Follow the model.

a. In our house, **we have** two personal computers.

In our house, there are two personal computers.

b. When my grandma was a child, **she had** only one black and white TV set in her house.

c. In our school, **we don't have** any computers in the classroom. **We have** computers in the lab.

d. This year, **I have** eight school subjects to study. Last year **I had** only seven.

Quick quiz – Let's talk!

According to Anatel (Agência Nacional de Telecomunicações), by April 2022 there were • **259,2 thousand** • **259,2 million** • **259,2 billion** mobile phones registered in Brazil.

Reamolko/Shutterstock.com/ID/BR

Available at https://informacoes.anatel.gov.br/paineis/acessos/telefonia-movel. Accessed on July 28, 2022.

Used to

1. Do you remember Doofus, from the *Reading corner* section? Look at what happened to him. Was it for better or for worse?

George Tutumi/ID/BR

Making sense

Look at the illustration above and write the correct answer in your notebook. Based on what Doofus is saying, we can affirm that:

a. the first sentence refers to a **I** (**present** / **past**) routine.

b. the second sentence refers to a **II** (**present** / **past**) routine.

c. we apply the form **used to** to talk about things that we **III** (**still do** / **don't do anymore**).

2. Talk to your parents or grandparents and complete these sentences in your notebook.

a. To listen to music, they used to...

b. To take pictures, they used to...

c. To talk to people in distant places, they didn't used to...

Go to **Grammar reference** (unit 5).

Open your ears

A short talk about tips on how to find friends on the Internet

1. Talk about these questions with a classmate.

a. Do you have friends on the Internet?

b. Do you interact with them in English?

Suryara Bernardi/ID/BR

2. Read the sentences and decide which expression in the box is true for you in each case. Discuss your ideas with a classmate.

a. There are no risks when chatting to people on the web, because they are far away.

I agree.	I disagree.	I am not sure.

b. Finding friends on the web is a good way to practice different languages.

I agree.	I disagree.	I am not sure.

c. It is a good idea to use a nickname to protect our identity.

I agree.	I disagree.	I am not sure.

d. We can give our phone number if we are talking to people from other countries.

I agree.	I disagree.	I am not sure.

e. If the conversation becomes uncomfortable, we should stop contact and let our teachers or parents know about it.

I agree.	I disagree.	I am not sure.

f. Having friends in other countries helps us learn a lot about other cultures.

I agree.	I disagree.	I am not sure.

15 3. Now listen to someone talking about making friends. Do you think we can use offline strategies to make friends online? Answer in your notebook.

15 4. Listen to the recording again. In your notebook, write who you think might be talking.

A a teenager
B an educator
C a parent
D someone from the website
E a police officer

15 5. The speaker gives suggestions on how to make friends. Listen again and write in your notebook one or more examples of suggestions and pieces of advice.

6. What else could be included in the list you made in activity 5? Work in groups and come up with a few more possibilities.

Não escreva no livro.

Pen to paper

A report about cell phone etiquette

Pre-writing

1. You are going to write a report about the problems that the inappropriate use of cell phones can cause. It will also include some suggestions on how these problems could be solved. Read the poster on page 71 and, in your notebook, write about some problems that are common in your community. For example: *Many people in my neighborhood use their cell phones while driving.*

2. In your notebook, write two suggestions for each one of the actions below. Use **should/should not** in the first suggestion and affirmative or negative imperative in the second one.

   a. Action 1: to use cell phones while driving

   b. Action 2: to keep the ringer volume up while in the library

Follow these steps to create your report

1. Copy the report below in your notebook replacing the numbers with your own ideas.

Introduction

The objective of this report is to discuss **I** and suggest **II**.

Description of the situation

Today, almost everyone has a cell phone. Unfortunately, many people do not know how to use it appropriately. **III** (describe some of the problems).

Conclusions and suggestions

Cell phones are very important for people nowadays, but we have to learn how to use them. **IV** (give suggestions using **should/should not** or the Imperative).

Evaluate yourself

1. Leia seu relatório novamente e, no caderno, avalie os itens abaixo.

   a. Ele está bem informativo e com linguagem formal?

   b. Descrevi bem a situação e dei exemplos?

   c. Incluí boas sugestões na conclusão?

2. Revise seu texto e, no caderno, reescreva-o, se necessário.

Focus on culture

Tech tool for English studies

Technology Can Shape Language

Nmedia/Shutterstock.com/ID/BR

Any parent or teacher who has taught a child to read will tell you that interpreting a text involves two steps. The first step involves decoding and defining individual words. The second (and more important) step is being able to understand what those words mean when they are grouped together as sentences and paragraphs. [...]

Rewordify.com is a free online tool that helps improve students' reading comprehension in multiple ways.

First, a user pastes or imports text into a text box on the site. Rewordify then analyzes this text, looking for words and phrases that may be difficult to understand. Once the site locates difficult or problematic language, it replaces it with simpler words to aid students' understanding. The [site] includes multiple settings so that users can choose from several reading levels. Users can click on the replacement words to display either the original, more difficult language or individual words' definitions [...].

Students also have the option of reading the original and replaced words with built-in text-to-speech functionality for auditory reinforcement. [...]

Finally, Rewordify has a collection of classic literature (like Shakespeare's plays) and historic documents (like the Declaration of Independence) that students can access, read, and better understand by using the site's unique comprehension tools.

Jamie Martin. 5 Tech Tools that Help Improve Reading Comprehension.
Available at https://www.noodle.com/articles/5-tech-tools-to-aid-your-reading-comprehension. Accessed on March 10, 2022.

1. Read the text and talk about these questions with your colleagues in small groups.

a. Do you usually use the Internet to learn English?

b. What are good aspects of improving your English by Internet?

c. How does technological advances affect the way you study?

2. Interview some older people (your parents, relatives or friends) and try to find out the similarities and differences between the way they studied and the way you do. Write a short paragraph in your notebook describing what you found out.

Não escreva no livro.

Self-assessment

Reflect about your own learning

assessment · learning · reflect · autonomy · English · responsibility · feedback

Freepik/ID/BR

I do it with confidence.	I do it well.	I can get better.

1. Como você avalia seu aprendizado nesta unidade? Reflita.

a. Que parte da unidade (seção, texto, imagem, mensagem do tutor, etc.) mais lhe agradou? Por quê?

b. Qual foi a parte de que você menos gostou? Por quê?

c. Você se lembra de alguma coisa que viu nesta unidade e que o ajudou fora da aula de inglês?

2. O que você pode fazer para melhorar seu aprendizado de inglês? Observe as opções abaixo e pense a respeito delas.

- Ler mais.
- Fazer mais atividades.
- Solucionar dúvidas com o professor.
- Trocar ideias com os colegas.
- Ouvir músicas em inglês.
- Assistir a filmes em inglês com legendas.

Daniel M Ernst/Shutterstock.com/ID/BR

Não escreva no livro.

UNIT

6 Special days

In this unit you will be introduced to some of the most common special days in English-speaking countries as well as in Brazil. The main text focuses on one of the most popular Christmas figures around the world: Santa Claus. All over the unit you will be engaged in activities that feature the following elements:

- **Genres:** magazine interview; invitation for a birthday party
- **Vocabulary:** special days; months; ordinal numbers
- **Grammar:** question words

Quick challenge

Read the questions below. Scan the pages of unit 6 and write the answers in your notebook.

a. What are the colors used in the title of the text in the *Reading corner* section?

b. How many birthday invitations are there on page 92?

c. What are the two email addresses in *Words, words, words (1)*?

d. One of these pictures is not used in this unit. Which one?

1
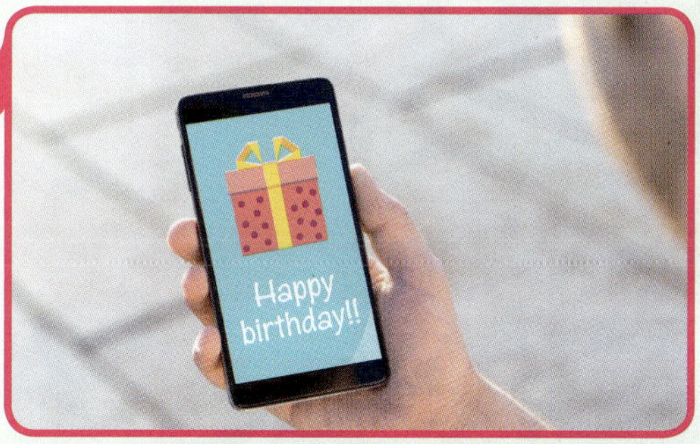

Photo: Preto Perola/Shutterstock.com/ID/BR; illustration: YANCOM/ID/BR

3

Chepko Danil Vitalevich/Shutterstock.com/ID/BR

2

Ampueroleonardo/iStock/Getty Images

4

Graphorama/ID/BR

A first approach

Talking about the topic

1. What special days are associated to these images?
2. Does everybody celebrate these dates the way it is represented in these images? What aspects can vary?
3. Are all of these special days celebrated in Brazil? Which one/ones is/are not very common?
4. What other events would you include here?

1

Volha Vasilevich/Shutterstock.com/ID/BR

4

Alexander Raths/Shutterstock.com/ID/BR

2

Lasko Dmitry/Shutterstock.com/ID/BR

5

Evgeny Karandaev/Shutterstock.com/ID/BR

3

Comzeal images/Shutterstock.com/ID/BR

6

Chepko Danil Vitalevich/Shutterstock.com/ID/BR

Não escreva no livro.

Exploring the topic

1. Match all the previous pictures with the celebrations below and write the combinations in your notebook. Six dates won't be used!

birthday	Carnival	Christmas	Easter
Earth Day	Halloween	Valentine's Day	Rosh Hashanah
Thanksgiving Day	New Year's Day	Independence Day	Labor Day

2. Special days quiz: What occasions do these sentences refer to? Write the answers in your notebook.

   a. Many people eat chocolate eggs on this day, and many others decorate real eggs.

   b. To celebrate this date, people like to wear colorful costumes and dance in the streets, but it varies a lot according to the culture and country.

   c. On this day, people go to parties dressed up as skeletons, vampires and witches, among other typical costumes. Some religions ban this tradition.

   d. For this time of the year, many people decorate a tree in their houses, but many others only take the chance to travel. Many people think this is too commercial.

   e. This is the day when the Jewish people celebrate the beginning of a New Year.

Discussion point

- Há comemorações que são próprias de um país, mas que acabam se popularizando em outros lugares do mundo. O *Halloween*, por exemplo, é tipicamente estadunidense. No entanto, de alguns anos para cá, essa celebração se tornou popular entre muitos brasileiros. Você imagina o motivo disso? Você acha positiva ou negativa essa influência de outras culturas na nossa? Por quê?

Looking around

1. Which of the dates mentioned in activity 1 are celebrated by you and your family?

2. How do you celebrate them? Do you know people who do it differently?

3. In Brazil, a typical festivity in June is called "São João" in some regions, and "Festa Junina" in other regions. What do you know about this celebration? Are the customs the same?

Dictionary 16

costume *noun* UK /ˈkɒs.tjuːm/ US /ˈkaː.stuːm/

Definition: the set of clothes typical of a particular country or period of history, or suitable for a particular activity.

Available at http://dictionary.cambridge.org/dictionary/british/costume?q=costume. Accessed on March 15, 2022.

Não escreva no livro.

Words, words, words (1)

Words related to special days

1. All these words are related to the special days of the previous section. Write in your notebook the words and expressions which you already know.

I bunny	VII square dance	XIII flag
II ghosts	VIII tambourine	XIV Santa (Claus)
III stocking	IX carol	XV gift
IV Trick or treat!	X pumpkin pie	XVI parades
V card	XI firework	XVII masks
VI turkey	XII drums	XVIII egg

2. Talk to your classmates. Compare the words you know to the words they know. If there are words in common you don't understand, use a dictionary.

3. Read the email below. A Brazilian teenager is sending it to an American teenager. Complete the text using some words from activity 1.

New message

New Send Insert Print

From: betina@mymail.com

To: sid@mymail.com

Subject: re: School project on special days_Brazil vs USA

Hi Sid,

How are you? You asked me to help you with your school work on special days. Below are my answers, OK? I hope this will be useful for your project.

Halloween: Yes, in Brazil, lots of people celebrate it as well. Many schools and night clubs promote parties where people go dressed up as witches or A like in your country. But it's not common to have kids knocking on people's door saying B.

Christmas: The figure of C is very common here, just like in your country. It wears red clothes, a long white beard and normally appears near the reindeer and snow, although December is a very hot month in Brazil 🙂.

Independence Day: Ours is on September 7th and it's also common to have D on the streets. But, different from your tradition, it's not really common to see so many people wearing the picture of the national E on their clothes on this day.

Tell me if you still need some more information, OK? It's always a pleasure to help you. Say hello to everybody.

Um abração (a tight hug 😄),

Betina

JB/ID/BR

Não escreva no livro.

Reading corner

Pre-reading

1. Look at the text below and talk with your classmates about these questions.

a. What type of text is this?

b. What do the parts in pink and the parts in black refer to?

c. What is the objective of the paragraph that starts with "Side by side with..."?

d. Do you think this text is real or fictitious? Why (not)?

YANCOM/ID/BR

Exclusive interview: Mrs. Claus

Side by side with every great man is a great woman. Santa and his wife, Mrs. Claus, have a hectic schedule at this time of year, but we pulled a few strings and managed to get an interview with Mrs. Claus about life at Korvatunturi, their home in Finnish Lapland.

Sherwood/Shutterstock.com/ID/BR

Mrs. Claus and Santa Claus.

Three questions about Santa

1. How old is Santa Claus?

That's something not even he can remember exactly. Once when he was sitting in his favourite rocking chair in front of the fireplace at Korvatunturi, the mountain in Finnish Lapland where our home is, he began to count how many Christmases he could remember. But when he got to something like 364, he fell asleep.

2. Does Santa Claus have to be good?

Santa Claus is always good. Sometimes he has to be strict, but he is always fair. Sometimes he's a little angry, sad or upset. He gets really upset if he hears about places in the world where they don't care for children's well-being.

3. Was Santa Claus ever a child, and did he go to school?

Santa Claus still feels like a child to this day. Life has been one long education for him. You have to keep studying because the world's always changing. He's gone to a lot of schools. Once he even visited an elementary school.

Dictionary 17

rocking chair *noun* UK /ˈrɒk.ɪŋ ˌtʃeər/ US /ˈrɑː.kɪŋ ˌtʃer/

Definition: a chair built on two pieces of curved wood so that it moves forwards and backwards when you are sitting in it.

Available at https://dictionary.cambridge.org/dictionary/english/rocking-chair. Accessed on May 3, 2022.

Adapted from https://finland.fi/christmas/exclusive-interview-mrs-claus/. Accessed on March 15, 2022.

Claudio Chiyo/ID/BR

Há muitos tipos de entrevista, e cada um tem características próprias. Além de entrevistas jornalísticas, há entrevistas de emprego, entrevistas de *talk show*, entre outros tipos. Elas variam no formato e nos objetivos (algumas são feitas para serem lidas; outras, para serem ouvidas; outras, para serem ouvidas e vistas), mas todas se constituem de perguntas e respostas.

Exploring the text

1. Look at these pictures. Match each illustration to its corresponding answer in the interview. Write the combination in your notebook.

A

B

C

Illustrations: Claudio Chiyo/ID/BR

2. In an interview, the answers are not necessarily objective all the time. Read the text on the previous page and check how Mrs. Claus reacts to some questions. Then, read the questions below and answer them in your notebook.

   a. When the interviewer asks Mrs. Claus "Does Santa Claus have to be good?",

      I she immediately answers "Yes, he does" and then she tells the reason.

      II she doesn't say "yes", but agrees, and includes other things.

      III she doesn't indicate if the answer is "yes" or "no". Her answer is vague.

   b. When the interviewer asks "How old is Santa Claus?",

      I she immediately tells how old he is.

      II she first tells a story and then she answers exactly how old he is.

      III she tells a story but she doesn't really answer how old he is.

3. In a real interview, marks of hesitation are very common. This occurs when the interviewees say, for example, "Well...", "You know...", "Actually...", "like..." or "hum..." as they talk. Act out the interview with Mrs. Claus adding some hesitations wherever you find appropriate.

Post-reading

1. Do you think the author of this fictitious interview was creative? Why (not)?

2. Do you think someone could believe this interview is real? Explain.

3. In Brazil, December is a very hot month. In your opinion, is the traditional image of Santa Claus appropriate for our culture?

Não escreva no livro.

Words, words, words (2)

Months

1. Look at the chart and at the words in the box below it. Then, copy the sentences from **a** to **d** in your notebook matching each date to its corresponding celebration.

Brazilian Special Days

Month	Special day
January	New Year's Day (1)
February	Carnival[MH] 
March	International Women's Day (8), Carnival[MH], Easter[MH]
April	Indian's Day (19), "Tiradentes" (21), Earth Day (22), Easter[MH]  
May	Labor Day (1), Mother's Day (2nd Sunday) 
June	Valentine's Day (12)
July	
August	Father's Day (2nd Sunday)
September	Independence Day (7)
October	Children's Day (12), Teacher's Day (15)  
November	Day of the Dead (2), Republic Day (15), Flag Day (19), Black Consciousness Day (20)
December	Christmas (25)

Illustrations: Graphorama/ID/BR

[MH] Movable Holiday

first	second	third	fourth	fifth	sixth
seventh	eighth	ninth	tenth	eleventh	twelfth

a. This special date is celebrated on the **I** Sunday in May in Brazil. It's **II**.

b. This special date is celebrated on the **III** Sunday in August in Brazil. It's **IV**.

c. This special date is celebrated in December, the **V** month of the year. It's **VI**.

d. This special date is celebrated on the **VII** day in September in Brazil. It's **VIII**.

2. In your notebook, write other sentences similar to the ones above. Ask your classmates to guess the special dates. Remember to include celebrations that are popular in your region.

3. Now discuss: What is the advantage of creating a calendar in English? In your opinion, which of the Brazilian festivities is more popular in other countries? Why?

Não escreva no livro.

Grammar bits

Question words

1. Look at the text below. What is this? Do you ever write this kind of text? Answer in your notebook.

YANCOM/ID/BR

DON'T SAY NO!!!
I'LL BE WAITING FOR U!!!

WHY? I'll turn 14!

WHEN? Saturday, November 4th

WHERE? My place: 14, Mahogany Street

WHAT TIME? 7pm

HOW TO GET THERE? See map on the back!

WHAT TO WEAR? Plaid (boys included)

XXX Alicia

Somyot Pattana/Shutterstock.com/ID/BR

Freepik/ID/BR

2. In your notebook, answer these questions according to the text above.

a. Who wrote this text?

b. Who is going to read it?

c. Why did she write it?

d. What does she say about clothes?

e. Where is everybody going to meet?

Making sense

Look at the invitation above and the questions in activity 2. Then, complete these sentences.

a. The question word used to ask about places is **I**.

b. The question word used to ask about people is **II**.

c. The question word used to ask for reasons is **III**.

Go to **Grammar reference** (unit 6).

A comemoração da data de nascimento varia de cultura para cultura. Enquanto alguns fazem festas com docinhos e bolos, outros consideram essa data como um rito de passagem. Como isso acontece na sua cultura? Você conhece outra forma de comemorar o aniversário de nascimento?

Claudio Chiyo/ID/BR

Open your ears

1. Look at these different ways to greet a person on a special day when you are not near. Which of them have you already used? In your opinion, which one is more effective and which one is less effective?

1

Aaron Amat/Shutterstock.com/ID/BR

2

oliveromg/Shutterstock.com/ID/BR

3

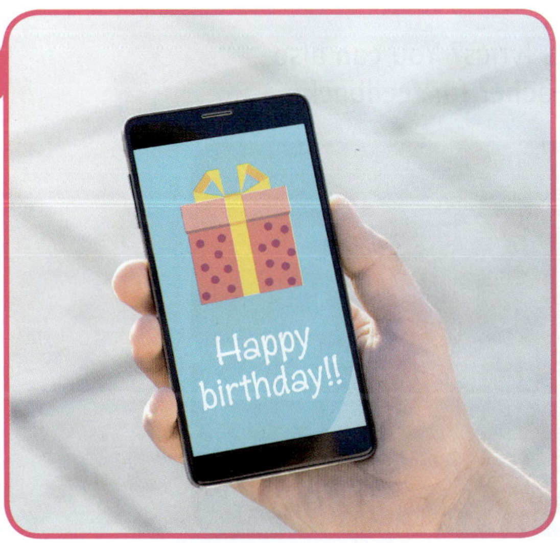

Photo: Preto Perola/Shutterstock.com/ID/BR; illustration: YANCOM/ID/BR

4

David MG/Shutterstock.com/ID/BR

5

Fernando Favoretto/Criar Imagem

6

VGstockstudio/Shutterstock.com/ID/BR

Não escreva no livro.

18 **2.** Listen to the song. Then, write in your notebook which of the ways below the singer is using to communicate his feelings.

I sending flowers

II sending an e-card

III sending an email

IV calling on the phone

V sending a letter

VI speaking face to face

18 **3.** Listen to the song again. In your notebook, make a chart like the one below and fill it with as many words as you can from the song. Then, compare your answers with a classmate's.

Months	Days of the week	Special days	Food	Seasons
||||||||||||||||	||||||||||||||||	||||||||||||||||	||||||||||||||||	||||||||||||||||

18 **4.** Read the sentences below. Then, listen to the song again and copy in your notebook the sentences that are true for you. Compare your ideas with a classmate's.

a. I think this song is interesting.

b. I think this song is beautiful.

c. I think this song is OK, not bad.

d. I like old songs, but this one is not my style.

e. I prefer other type of music.

f. I would dedicate this song to my mother.

g. This song makes me feel happy.

h. I think the words of this song are very powerful.

5. If you liked this song, why don't you search for its lyrics? You can also translate it into Portuguese and give it to your teacher for feedback.

Quick quiz – Let's talk!

The singer who first recorded the song you heard in these activities is very famous and talented. Do you know his name? He sings, writes songs, produces records, and plays different instruments as well. Being blind doesn't stop him from doing all these things. Look at this picture. The musical instrument he is playing is:

accordion • xylophone • keyboard

Kevin Mazur/Getty Images

Não escreva no livro.

Speaker's corner

Role-playing

1. Look at these pictures. What do you think is happening in each situation?

Illustrations: Graphorama/ID/BR

2. The following sentences are parts of the conversations represented in the pictures above. Write the appropriate combination of letters-numbers in your notebook.

I **A:** Harumi?

B: Yeah, that's me.

A: Hi, this is Pedro... I need a favor. Could you help me?

II **A:** Oh, Lisa. I was absent last class. Can you help me with these questions?

B: Yeah. What do you want to know, Becky?

3. Role-play these situations with a classmate. Then, switch roles and change partner.

STUDENT A

Situation 1

You were invited for the birthday party of a classmate. The problem is: You lost the invitation! You want to go to the party. Your cousin has the invitation and he/she can give you the details. Call your cousin, explain the situation, and ask about the day of the party, the time, the place, how to get there, and the clothes to wear.

Situation 2

You missed last History class and now you can't study for a test you will have in two hours. You don't have time to search the Internet or go to the library. Your classmate can help you. Talk to him or her, explain the situation, and then ask when Independence Day is celebrated in the following countries: India, the USA, Cuba, Mexico, and Colombia.

STUDENT B

Situation 1

You were invited for the birthday party of a classmate. Your cousin wants to go, but he/she lost the invitation. You have the invitation. Your cousin is calling you to get the information: The party is on Friday, November 11th. Time: 8pm. Place: Strike Club, on Miami Street. People can get there by taking Bus 75. Everybody should wear a nice hat, black T-shirt, and jeans.

Situation 2

Your classmate badly needs your help because he or she has to study for a test. You have all the notes your classmate needs. Your classmate wants to know when Independence Day is celebrated in some countries. Help him or her. Independence Day in Argentina: July 9th; in India: August 15th; in the USA: July 4th; in Jamaica: August 6th; in Cuba: May 20th; in Colombia: July 20th; in Mexico: September 16th.

Pen to paper

Writing an invitation for a birthday party

Pre-writing

1. Read these invitations. Write in your notebook the kind of party related to each one.

1

2

3

Illustrations: Graphorama/ID/BR

2. Write in your notebook which piece of information below is missing in the invitations.

I Name of the person/people giving the party.

II How old the person/people will be.

III The day and time of the party.

IV The place where the party will be.

V What kind of party it will be.

VI Regrets*

* This word means you should only call if you can't go.

Follow these steps to write your invitation

1. Get ready to create a paper invitation for your next birthday. Consider your friends that study English. In your notebook, write a first draft. Look at the invitations above for ideas.

2. Decide the kind of invitation you want it to be. Consider the layout, the type and size of fonts, the pictures (photos, illustrations), the shape (rectangular, square, circular, etc.) and the colors.

3. Now it's time to get to work. Get a piece of card and create a final version of your invitation.

Evaluate yourself

1. Reveja o convite que você criou e avalie os itens abaixo.

a. As informações estão bem distribuídas no convite?

I Sim. II Não.

b. A pessoa que receber o convite terá todas as informações necessárias para comparecer à festa?

I Sim. II Não. III Sim, mas ainda posso fornecer mais detalhes.

2. Reescreva seu texto, se necessário.

Não escreva no livro.

A thankful day

THANKSGIVING TRADITIONS

Illustrations: YANCOM/ID/BR

Each year Americans in the United States celebrate the Thanksgiving holiday on the fourth Thursday of November. Most families follow traditions begun on the first Thanksgiving, but many have their own traditions that they follow each year. [...]

Travel

One of the best things about Thanksgiving is spending time with family. Many people live far from family members and travel long distances by car, train, or plane to be with their loved ones. Thanksgiving is the busiest travel day of the year!

The Feast

Traditional foods are a large part of Thanksgiving celebrations. Many families include the entire family in the food preparation. Traditional foods include turkey, stuffing, gravy, sweet potatoes, cornbread, mashed potatoes, and cranberry sauce. Many people serve pie for dessert at the end of the meal. Popular pie flavors are pumpkin, pecan, sweet potato, and apple.

Vegetarian Foods

Some families choose to serve vegetarian Thanksgiving dinners instead of a stuffed turkey. Some people eat vegetarian turkey, which is made out of tofu. Others prefer to eat squash, salads, or other fruit and vegetable dishes.

[...]

Ariel Skelley/DigitalVision/Getty Images

Helping Others

Many generous folks use Thanksgiving as an opportunity to help the less fortunate. Some people volunteer to serve food at homeless shelters on Thanksgiving Day and others donate to shelters [...].

After the Meal

After the feast families often do additional activities. Some like to take walks after eating such a large meal. Some people take naps. Others sit down together to play board or card games together.

Adapted from https://kids.nationalgeographic.com/explore/history/thanksgiving-traditions/. Accessed on March 15, 2022.

1. Thanksgiving is a special date that was commemorated for the first time in 1621 in the United States, by the Pilgrims. The feast was made to celebrate the successful harvest after a harsh winter. Now, it is an occasion that motivates people to reflect about what they are thankful for. Discuss with your classmates: What are you thankful for?

2. In Brazil, it's not common to celebrate Thanksgiving. Do you think that it would be important to celebrate this holiday? Why (not)?

3. In groups, do some research about holidays in others countries and how people celebrate them. Choose one and make a poster to present to the class.

Self-assessment

Reflect about your own learning

Freepik/ID/BR

I do it with confidence.	I do it well.	I can get better.

1. Como você avalia seu aprendizado nesta unidade? Reflita.

a. Que parte da unidade (seção, texto, imagem, mensagem do tutor, etc.) mais lhe agradou? Por quê?

b. Qual foi a parte de que você menos gostou? Por quê?

c. Você se lembra de alguma coisa que viu nesta unidade e que o ajudou fora da aula de inglês?

2. O que você pode fazer para melhorar seu aprendizado de inglês? Observe as opções abaixo e pense a respeito delas.

- Ler mais.
- Fazer mais atividades.
- Solucionar dúvidas com o professor.
- Trocar ideias com os colegas.
- Ouvir músicas em inglês.
- Assistir a filmes em inglês com legendas.

Evgeny Karandaev/Shutterstock.com/ID/BR

Não escreva no livro.

UNIT

7 Changes

In this unit you will be dealing with activities that will make you think, learn, and reflect about an important topic in life: change. The main text focuses on the experience of a girl studying abroad. All over the unit you will be engaged in activities that feature the following elements:

- **Genres:** article; oral presentation
- **Vocabulary:** parts of a house
- **Grammar:** *Going to*; Simple future

Quick challenge

Read the questions below. Scan the pages of unit 7 and write the answers in your notebook.

a. What is the topic of the section *Words, words, words*?

b. One of these pictures is not used in this unit. Which one?

1

Africa Studio/Shutterstock.com/ID/BR

3

Jana Shea/Shutterstock.com/ID/BR

2

Ruddy Gold/Easypix Brasil

4

NemesisINC/Shutterstock.com/ID/BR

Não escreva no livro.

A first approach

Talking about the topic

1. What is the connection between these images and the title of the unit?
2. Which of these situations have you already experienced?
3. Do you still live in the same city you were born in?
4. How many schools have you studied in? Do you like experiencing new situations in life?

1

Jana Shea/Shutterstock.com/ID/BR

5

EKA Collection/Easypix Brasil

2

Bernard Jaubert/Easypix Brasil

6

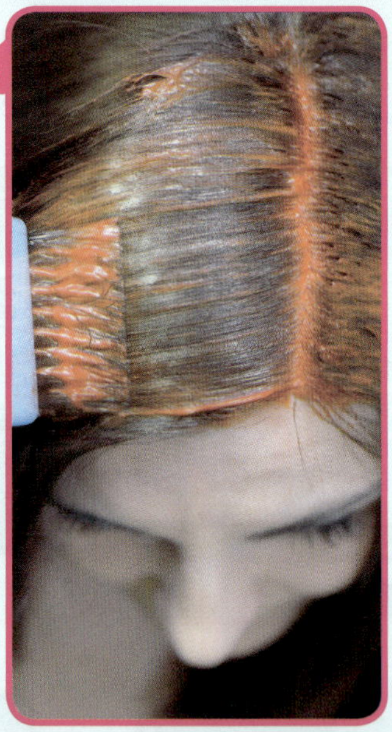

Stock Photography/Shutterstock.com/ID/BR

7

Abo Photography/Shutterstock.com/ID/BR

3

Ruddy Gold/Easypix Brasil

4

Fernando Favoretto/ID/BR

8

Spencer Platt/Getty Images

Exploring the topic

1. Read the sentences below and copy into your notebook the ones that are true for you.

ARE YOU ALWAYS LOOKING FOR A CHANGE IN YOUR LIFE?

1. I change my dressing style all the time.
2. I always have the same hair cut.
3. If I could, I would study in a different school every year.
4. When I go to a restaurant, I always order the same food.
5. I think it's boring to live in the same place all your life.
6. I am always making new friends. I love meeting new people.
7. I have one or two favorite bands/singers and I only listen to their music.

2. Talk to a classmate. Did you choose the same sentences? Discuss your answers and give reasons.
3. Read the sentences of the quiz again and answer the questions below in your notebook.
   a. Which sentences would people who like changes probably choose?
   b. Which sentences would people who don't like changes probably choose?
4. Talk to your classmate again. Who likes changes the most: you or your classmate?

Looking around

1. What are the pros and cons of moving to a different city, state, or country?
2. Some people are constantly moving. Look at the picture on the right. Who else, besides this kind of people, can you think of?
3. Some other people experience physical changes very often. Do you think they like this "routine"?

1000 Words/Shutterstock.com/ID/BR

Gabriel Olsen/FilmMagic/Ojo+/Getty Images

Rodrigo Santoro is an actor that has changed his look several times.

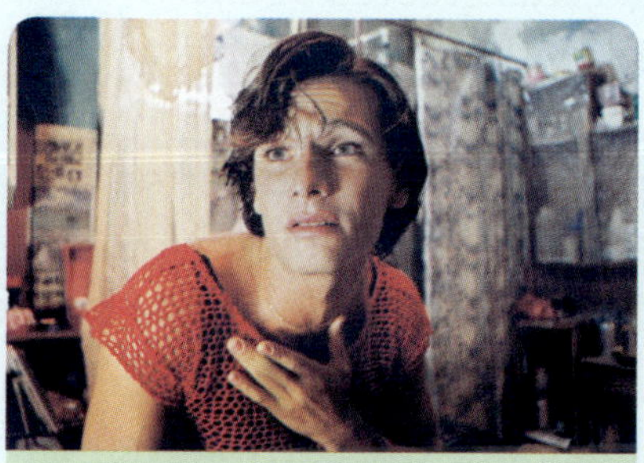

Sony Pictures/Everett Collection/Fotoarena

Lady Di, in *Carandiru*. Direction: Hector Babenco. Brazil: Columbia Tristar, 2003.

Warner Bros/Everett Collection/Fotoarena

Imperor Xerxes, in *300*. Direction: Zack Snyder. USA: Warner Bros, 2006.

Não escreva no livro.

Reading corner

Pre-reading

1. Imagine you are going to study in a different country. What would you worry about? In your notebook, write the options that are true for you. You can add other ideas to the list.

I would worry about...

a. ... my new house.
b. ... my new school.
c. ... my new teachers.
d. ... difficulties in communicating with other people.
e. ... missing my friends.
f. ... finding nice places to go.
g. ... the kind of food there.
h. ... the weather there.

Exploring the text

1. Read Grace's description of her experience abroad as a language student and an English language assistant. Which items in activity 1 above are mentioned in the text? Write the answer in your notebook.

Liravega/Shutterstock.com/ID/BR

Learning to adapt

by: GraceL

JGI/Jamie Grill/Blend Images/Getty Images

So I moved to Nordenham in Lower Saxony, Germany, about a month ago for my year abroad. I am working as a foreign language assistant in a school here. At university I study German, so naturally, my aim is to improve my German this year. Before I came, I was very nervous that I would not understand what anyone said. This made moving away from England quite scary at first. From the moment I arrived in Germany, everything seemed so different but so exciting. I was greeted at the train station by a teacher from the school I work at who drove me to the people I was staying with. As we arrived the table was already set with coffee and amazing cakes! Coffee and cake is something of a tradition in Germany, like afternoon tea in England! I knew this was going to be the start of a great year.

I am very open to new things and to changes so I soon adapted to the German way of life. The hardest change was the early starts! The first lesson in my school starts at 7:35 which is much earlier than in England so I have to make sure I go to bed earlier so that I'm not too tired. Another difference is that in Germany, people tend to eat a big meal at lunchtime and then something smaller in the evening. In England we usually eat something small at lunchtime and then a larger meal in the evening. I also noticed that lots of Germans seem to wear scarves, especially in northern Germany where it can be quite cold! I was told by a teacher at my school that I would not survive here without a scarf so I quickly bought one.

I love the way that schools start earlier and finish earlier here. When the school day finishes at 1 pm it is really nice to have some free time for the rest of the day. I like to go cycling or for walks on the beach. I have noticed that cycling is extremely popular in Germany! I really enjoy it so it has been easy for me to adapt and travel everywhere by bike.

Thanks for reading, till next time!

Available at http://learnenglishteens.britishcouncil.org/magazine/life-around-world/learning-adapt/. Accessed on March 10, 2022.

Liravega/Shutterstock.com/ID/BR

2. Look at these statements. Are these facts mentioned in the article? Read the text again and correct the false statements in your notebook.

a. Different from England, school classes start late in Germany.

b. Grace likes to spend her free time driving around the city.

c. It was difficult for her to get used to the German way of life.

d. She thought people wouldn't understand what she said.

e. German people usually wear scarves in the winter.

f. In Germany people usually have tea and cake in the afternoon.

g. English people often have a big meal for lunch and something smaller in the evening.

A atividade 2 pede que você verifique se as sentenças são verdadeiras ou falsas. Esse tipo de exercício é útil porque leva você a comparar dois textos para verificar se eles expressam ideias parecidas. Essa prática de leitura é particularmente interessante no contato com uma língua estrangeira, pois há vocabulário novo envolvido e você tem de ficar atento a antônimos, sinônimos, etc. Isso mostra também que, em todo idioma, há sempre várias maneiras de expressar uma mesma ideia.

Claudio Chiyo/ID/BR

Dictionary 19

scarf *noun* [C] UK /skɑːf/ US /skɑːrf/ plural: scarves or scarfs

Definition: a strip, square, or triangle of cloth, worn around the neck, head, or shoulders to keep you warm or to make you look attractive.

Available at https://dictionary.cambridge.org/pt/dicionario/ingles/scarf. Accessed on March 10, 2022.

Post-reading

1. If you were Grace, what would you enjoy the most in your "new life"?

2. What would you miss the most?

3. Now, imagine you received a scholarship to study abroad. Where are you going to study? Why would you choose this country?

Não escreva no livro.

Grammar bits (1)

Going to

1. Work in pairs. Read these article headlines and talk to your classmate what they are about.

1 IT'S HOT, BUT IT'S GOING TO GET EVEN HOTTER

Available at https://www.vrt.be/vrtnws/en/2018/07/22/it_s-hot-but-its-going-to-get-even-hotter/. Accessed on March 10, 2022.

2 "I LOVE IT, SO I'M GOING TO DO IT."

Available at https://www.washingtoncitypaper.com/arts/music/blog/13077136/jazz-vocalist-integriti-reeves-i-love-it-so-im-going-to-do-it. Accessed on March 10, 2022.

3 THE FUTURE OF TRAVEL: HOW TECHNOLOGY IS GOING TO CHANGE HOLIDAYS

Available at https://www.stuff.co.nz/travel/news/105041973/the-future-of-travel-how-technology-is-going-to-change-holidays. Accessed on March 10, 2022.

4 I THOUGHT, "I'M NOT GOING TO MAKE IT"
JONNY BROWNLEE TELLS THE BBC ABOUT BEING HELPED TO THE TRIATHLON FINISH LINE BY HIS BROTHER.

Available at https://www.bbc.com/news/av/uk-37415817/i-thought-i-m-not-going-to-make-it. Accessed on March 10, 2022.

5 *INSIGHT*: WHY I AM NOT GOING TO BUY A COMPUTER

Available at www.plough.com/en/topics/justice/sustainable-living/insight-why-i-am-not-going-to-buy-a-computer. Accessed on March 10, 2022.

6 FUTURE HEAT WAVES ARE GOING TO MAKE AIR TRAVEL A PAIN

Available at http://www.sciencemag.org/news/2017/07/future-heat-waves-are-going-make-air-travel-pain. Accessed on March 10, 2022.

Making sense

Based on the sentences above, choose the appropriate option that completes the statements below. Use your notebook to write the answers.

a. These sentences refer to events in the I (**past** / **present** / **future**).

b. In sentences 2 and 5, the verb form *going to* indicates II (**predictions about the future based on present evidence** / **near future plans and intentions**).

c. In sentences 1, 3, 4, and 6, the verb form *going to* expresses III (**predictions about the future based on present evidence** / **near future plans and intentions**).

d. To form a sentence with *going to*, we use the verb IV (**to do** / **to be**) in the present.

e. After *going to*, we use the main verb in the V (**infinitive** / **gerund**).

2. What's going to happen? Look at the images carefully and complete the sentences in your notebook using *going to*.

a. The man **I** fall in the manhole.

c. They **III** travel.

Illustrations: Suryara Bernardi/ID/BR

b. This person **II** slip on a banana peel.

d. They **IV** get married.

3. You are going to interview some of your classmates about their plans for the weekend. In your notebook, create a chart similar to the one below. Use the "Your classmate's answer" column to write what you've found out.

What are you going to do on the weekend?	
Your classmate's name	Your classmate's answer
João	going to the movies
Camila	not going to the club

4. Based on your interviews, talk to your classmates about the most popular and the least popular activity for the weekend.

Não escreva no livro.

Words, words, words

Parts of a house

1. Talk about these questions with a classmate.

a. Do you live in a house or in an apartment?

b. Can you describe it to me?

c. What is the best thing about it?

d. If you could, what would you change in your house or apartment?

2. Look at the details of some images. They all show parts of a house. Look carefully and write, in your notebook, the word corresponding to each part.

Whyframe/Shutterstock.com/ID/BR

Tapui/Shutterstock.com/ID/BR

Alice-Photo/Shutterstock.com/ID/BR

Francesco Scatena/Shutterstock.com/ID/BR

Paradise On Earth/Shutterstock.com/ID/BR

Antoha713/Shutterstock.com/ID/BR

Robophobic/Shutterstock.com/ID/BR

Africa Studio/Shutterstock.com/ID/BR

Ao interagir com alguém, é importante demonstrar interesse pelo que o interlocutor está dizendo. Você pode dizer, entre outras possibilidades: *That's interesting!* | *Tell me more about it.* | *Wow! Really?* | *Lucky you!* | *Great!* | *You're kidding!* | *Sorry (Nice) to hear that!* | *No way!*.

Claudio Chiyo/ID/BR

3. What elements in the pictures above helped you get to the answers? Talk to a classmate.

Não escreva no livro.

20 **4.** Listen to a father and son talking about doing housework. What parts of the house do they mention? Use your notebook to write the answers.

a. dining room
b. living room
c. laundry room
d. kitchen
e. home office
f. bathroom
g. bedroom
h. backyard
i. garage
j. family room
k. hall
l. garden

Claudia Marianno/ID/BR

5. Read this list of household chores. Do you know what they all mean? Write the translations in your notebook.

a. clean the bathroom
b. do the dishes
c. make the bed
d. pick up the toys
e. pull the weeds
f. set the table
g. take out the garbage
h. wash the clothes
i. do the cooking
j. dust the furniture
k. mop the floor
l. polish the furniture
m. rake the leaves
n. sweep the floor
o. vacuum the carpet
p. wipe the walls

20 **6.** Listen to the recording again and check the housework that the father (**F**) has to do and the housework that the son (**S**) has to do. Write **F** or **S** in your notebook according to what you hear.

7. In activity 5, some words are not necessarily transcriptions of the words you heard in the recording. What helped you choose the correct answers? Talk about it with your classmates.

Não escreva no livro.

Grammar bits (2)

Simple future

1. Read the text and answer the following questions in your notebook.

> On the first day of school, it will be terrifying, because rarely before in your life have you ever been in a situation where you literally don't know anyone. Make lots of friends. Ask anyone and everyone if you can eat lunch with them. People will be curious about who you are; introduce yourself, smile a lot and just act naturally. Sooner or later, you will find your people. (Or they'll find you.)
>
> Available at https://www.huffpost.com/entry/10-things-i-have-learned-_b_5527931. Accessed on March 10, 2022.

a. The text deals with the experience of taking good grades or making friends at a new school?

b. The sentence "People will be curious about who you are" refers to the past, to the present or to the future?

c. In the text, this sentence is used to express the idea of prediction, offer or promise?

d. Which other sentences in the text are similar to that one?

2. Read the three situations below and write in your notebook what you would say in each case. Look at the model.

Situation: You see a friend carrying two heavy bags. You decide to give him/her a hand.

Don't worry. I'll help you with the bags.

Situation A: Your friend tells you there's no more coffee. You decide to go out and buy some.

Situation B: You friend has just lent you some money.

Situation C: Your friend tells you a secret and asks you not to tell anybody.

Making sense

Read the sentences and choose the appropriate option. Write the answers in your notebook.

a. We use *will* + infinitive, or its contracted form *'ll*, to talk about an event in the **I** (**past** / **present** / **future**).

b. In situation A, what is said expresses the idea of **II** (**prediction** / **offer** / **promise**).

c. In situation B, what is said expresses the idea of **III** (**prediction** / **offer** / **promise**).

d. In situation C, what is said expresses the idea of **IV** (**prediction** / **offer** / **promise**).

e. The sentence "Sooner or later, you will find your people" expresses the idea of **V** (**prediction** / **offer** / **promise**).

21 **3.** Read the lyrics of the song on the next page and write in your notebook the words whose meaning you don't know. Then, listen to the song and sing along.

We're Going To Be Friends

White Stripes

Suryara Bernardi/ID/BR

Fall is here, hear the yell
Back to school, ring the bell
Brand new shoes, walking blues
Climb the fence, books and pens
I can tell that we are gonna be friends
I can tell that we are gonna be friends

Walk with me, Suzy Lee
Through the park and by the tree
We will rest upon the ground
And look at all the bugs we found
Safely walk to school without a sound
Safely walk to school without a sound

Here we are, no one else
We walked to school all by ourselves
There's dirt on our uniforms
From chasing all the ants and worms
We clean up and now it's time to learn
We clean up and now it's time to learn

Numbers, letters, learn to spell
Nouns, and books, and show and tell
Playtime we will throw the ball
Back to class, through the hall
Teacher marks our height against the wall
Teacher marks our height against the wall

We don't notice any time pass
We don't notice anything
We sit side by side in every class
Teacher thinks that I sound funny
But she likes the way you sing

Tonight I'll dream while I'm in bed
When silly thoughts go through my head
About the bugs and alphabet
And when I wake tomorrow I'll bet
That you and I will walk together again
I can tell that we are gonna be friends
I can tell that we are gonna be friends.

Available at https://www.azlyrics.com/lyrics/whitestripes/weregoingtobefriends.html. Accessed on March 10, 2022.

Em inglês, a forma *gonna* é muito usada na linguagem oral e nas músicas. É uma forma reduzida de *going to*, como na expressão *we are gonna be friends*. Às vezes, pode aparecer ainda mais reduzida, sem o verbo *to be*, como em *we gonna be friends*. Algo parecido acontece em português quando dizemos "né?" (não é?) e "tá bem?" (está bem?).

Claudio Chiyo/ID/BR

Não escreva no livro.

4. Read the questions below. Then, talk to a classmate about them.

a. Who is the "we" in the song?

b. How old are they?

c. What do they do before class?

d. Do you think they live in a big city? Why (not)?

5. Look at these images and find in the song the verses or expressions that can be related to them. Write the answers in your notebook.

A

Viacheslav Nikolaenko/Shutterstock.com/ID/BR

D

funky-data/Getty Images

B

Africa Studio/Shutterstock.com/ID/BR

E

DigitalVision/Getty Images

C

Radius Images/Getty Images

F

FamVeld/Shutterstock.com/ID/BR

6. Read the last stanza again and talk to your classmates about the following questions.

a. Some verses are in the Simple future. Which are they?

b. Do these verses express the idea of offer, prediction or promise?

c. Which is the verse that also appears at the end of the first stanza?

d. What idea does this verse express? Prediction about the future based on present evidence or near future plans and intentions?

e. Which verse expresses the idea that the speaker is very confident about the future?

Open your ears

1. Talk to a classmate about the questions below.

a. Is it easy for you to make new friends? Why?

b. What should we do to approach people and make friends?

Caiaimage/Sam Edwards/Ojo+/Getty Images

2. Here are some tips on how to make friends at a new school. Study them carefully and decide: Are they good tips? How could they help you?

a. You should be careful about what you tell your friends. Gossiping is the big thing.

b. Try to wear nice clothes and hair.

c. Not everyone you meet is your friend just because they're nice to you.

d. Smile at people.

e. Do not make someone stop being friends with someone else just because you don't like that.

f. Try not to call people your friends unless you've shared moments and are hanging out for a while and you feel you can trust them.

22 **3.** Listen to a girl giving advice on friendship at high school. Two of the tips in activity 2 were not mentioned. What are they? Write the letters in your notebook.

22 **4.** Listen to the beginning of the recording again and write the correct answer in your notebook. The speaker mentions that going to high school can be overwhelming because there are a lot of students. But, actually, that makes it easier to make...

trends	friends	complaints

22 **5.** Read the sentences below. Are they true (**T**) or false (**F**), according to what you can remember from the recording? Write the answers in your notebook. Then, listen again and check.

a. Teens form initial opinions of other teens based on what they wear, their hair style, and fashion sense.

b. You can hate someone one day and then the next day you guys are best friends.

c. Just because someone's nice to you or helps you out in some way it doesn't make them your friends. You have to get to know them.

d. If you do the right thing, you will certainly make a lot of new friends on Day 1.

Não escreva no livro.

Speaker's corner

A presentation to new students at a school

1. You are going to prepare a short presentation to new students arriving at your school. First, make a list in your notebook of important things new students should know, such as: times and schedules; different subjects; facilities available for the students (sports court, cafeteria, library, computer lab, etc.); important rules they have to know; social activities (parties, trips, etc.).

Claudia Marianno/ID/BR

2. Think about the type of language you will use. Here are some examples for your reference. Just match the following words to the sentences below in your notebook.

I Classes...	**III** Football practice...	**V** There are...	**VII** There is...
II You can...	**IV** You have to...	**VI** You must...	**VIII** You should...

A ... a library in the school.

B ... bring something to eat during the break. If you don't, you may feel hungry.

C ... do all your homework. Teachers get angry if you don't.

D ... finish(es) at 4 pm.

E ... start(s) at 7:15 every day.

F ... take part in sports competitions, if you like.

G ... three math lessons every week.

3. Decide on the order you want to present the topics. Write your presentation in a sheet of paper and give it to your teacher to check before your speech.

4. Now, make your presentation to the class. Good luck!

Para iniciar sua apresentação oral, você pode usar:
I'm going to talk about...
The main focus of this presentation is...

Quando você precisar ordenar suas ideias, é possível usar:

Let's start with...	*Secondly...*	*Finally...*
First of all...	*Next...*	*Lastly...*
Firstly...	*Then...*	*In conclusion...*

Claudio Chiyo/ID/BR

Pen to paper

Writing in a blog about changes and your plans for the future

Pre-writing

1. Many websites give visitors the opportunity to post their comments there. Why do website producers make this possible? Choose answers from the ideas below. Answer in your notebook.

a. They think visitors will spend more time exploring the website.

b. They really want to know how visitors react to the contents of the website.

c. They only want to offer visitors the chance to be famous on web.

d. They do it because they know that people are curious and like to know what other visitors think about the same theme.

2. The theme of the following text is "changes". Read it and talk about the questions below to your classmates.

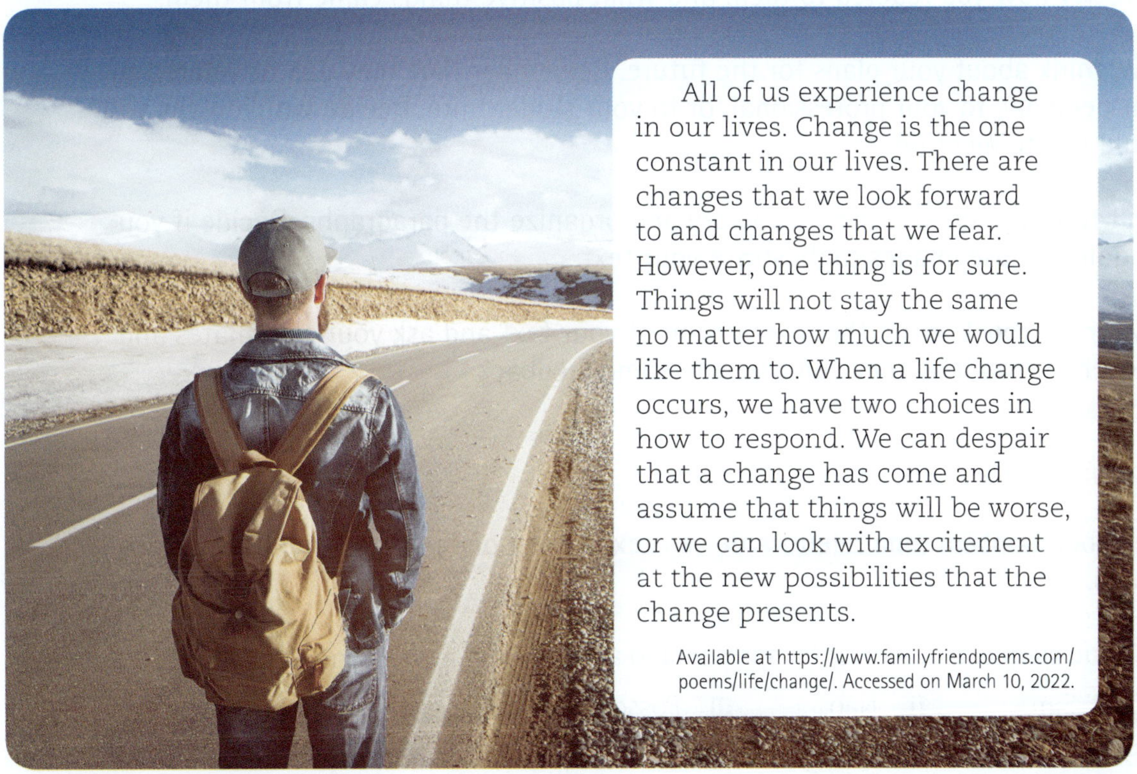

Yanik88/Shutterstock.com/ID/BR

All of us experience change in our lives. Change is the one constant in our lives. There are changes that we look forward to and changes that we fear. However, one thing is for sure. Things will not stay the same no matter how much we would like them to. When a life change occurs, we have two choices in how to respond. We can despair that a change has come and assume that things will be worse, or we can look with excitement at the new possibilities that the change presents.

Available at https://www.familyfriendpoems.com/poems/life/change/. Accessed on March 10, 2022.

a. Do you agree with it? Why?

b. Do you think changes are important in our lives or it would be better if everything stayed the same?

c. In your opinion, which changes are welcome and which are not welcome?

d. If you could change anything in your life, what would it be?

Follow these steps to write your blog post

1. Imagine you are going to write a blog post talking about changes you have experienced and your plans for the future. First, think about changes in your life and answer the questions below in your notebook.
   a. What were some of the significant changes in your life?
   b. How did you react to these changes?
   c. What positive things came from them?
   d. What are your plans for the future?

Pekic/E+/Getty Images

2. Decide if you want to write about one change only or more than one. Think about the details you want to include. In your notebook, make a list of these details.
3. Write in your notebook an introductory sentence before you describe the changes Then, say how you reacted to them and what positive things came from them.
4. Now, think about your plans for the future. Remember that they can be related to your personal, to your professional, or to your student life. Decide which plans you would like to mention.
5. Don't forget to choose the vocabulary and organize the paragraphs. Decide if you are going to use images to illustrate your text.
6. In your notebook, write the first version of your text and ask your classmates and teacher to read it so they can give you some feedback.

Evaluate yourself

1. Faça você também uma releitura de seu texto e responda no caderno às questões abaixo.
   a. O que eu queria descrever foi apresentado ao leitor de forma interessante?
      I Sim. II Não. III Posso tornar a descrição mais interessante.
   b. Descrevi a forma como reagi e relatei as consequências da mudança?
      I Sim. II Não. III Posso tornar a descrição mais detalhada.
   c. Meu texto está adequado para ser postado em um *site* ou blogue?
      I Sim. II Não.
2. Reescreva seu texto, se necessário. Use o caderno.

Não escreva no livro.

Focus on culture

Music and culture

1. Look at the image and the title of this article and talk to your classmates: What do you know about The Beatles? What are your favorite Beatles' songs?

2. Now, read the text and talk about the following questions.

When The Beatles Changed Everything

CBS Photo Archive/CBS/Getty Images

The Beatles on *The Ed Sullivan Show*, New York, 1964.

Thenatchdl/Shutterstock.com/ID/BR

When John, Paul, George and Ringo stepped off the plane at New York's John F. Kennedy International Airport on Feb. 7, 1964, they had no idea they were making history. Despite their reception, they were still a mystery to MOST of America, until two days later, when Ed Sullivan made the introductions: "Ladies and gentleman... The Beatles!" An astonishing 73 million Americans tuned in that night – nearly 40 percent of the U.S. population. [...]

Steven Stark was one of the millions whose lives changed that night, so much so that 30 years later he moved his family from Boston to Liverpool to write a book about exactly how The Beatles changed everything.

"Rock music was not the soundtrack to a generation, it WAS the generation," Stark said. "It was the air, it was considered to be the central, and a revolutionary and new – kind of the way the people think of the Internet is now – communication force that would change everything. It would change our politics, our culture, our fashion, and The Beatles were the crown princes of this movement." [...]

Whatever fans were getting from The Beatles, it all starts with the songs. From 1962 through their breakup in 1970, they would write roughly 200 of them. Then there were the films, the changing hairstyles, and most importantly, the ever-evolving music. "Most pop culture figures become well-known, and then they stop growing," said Stark. "They keep doing what got them there. The Beatles constantly reinvent themselves. They don't want to keep doing the same thing even more than once, and in a way as they reinvent themselves, they reinvent all of their followers – and we're talking hundreds of millions." [...]

"I think people recognize in The Beatles today, younger people, a feeling of hope and optimism that people miss," said Stark. "They miss the excitement of the time, the idea that you are on the ground making history is a very heady feeling, and they wish they had it."

Available at https://www.cbsnews.com/news/when-the-beatles-changed-everything/. Accessed on March 10, 2022.

a. According to the text, the changes brought by The Beatles were significant to society. Do you agree with that? Why?

b. In your opinion, are The Beatles the biggest rock and roll stars of all times? Who else would you choose?

3. In groups, research about The Beatles' influence in Brazil. Make a presentation to the class.

Não escreva no livro.

Self-assessment

Reflect about your own learning

assessment | learning | reflect | autonomy

English | responsibility | feedback

Freepik/ID/BR

I do it with confidence.	I do it well.	I can get better.

1. Como você avalia seu aprendizado nesta unidade? Reflita.

a. Que parte da unidade (seção, texto, imagem, mensagem do tutor, etc.) mais lhe agradou? Por quê?

b. Qual foi a parte de que você menos gostou? Por quê?

c. Você se lembra de alguma coisa que viu nesta unidade e que o ajudou fora da aula de inglês?

2. O que você pode fazer para melhorar seu aprendizado de inglês? Observe as opções abaixo e pense a respeito delas.

- Ler mais.
- Fazer mais atividades.
- Solucionar dúvidas com o professor.
- Trocar ideias com os colegas.
- Ouvir músicas em inglês.
- Assistir a filmes em inglês com legendas.

Samuel Borges Photography/Shutterstock.com/ID/BR

Não escreva no livro.

UNIT 8 Literature for life

In this unit you are going to read and explore extracts from different genres of literary work. You will learn vocabulary and other linguistic items by doing activities based on literature. The main text gives you the opportunity to read the passages of three different genres in English. All over the unit you will be engaged in activities that feature the following elements:

- **Genres:** poem; fiction (novel); fairy tale
- **Vocabulary:** words related to library
- **Grammar:** Present perfect

Quick challenge

Look at the instructions below. Go through the pages of unit 8 and answer the following questions in your notebook.

a. Find a book cover with a funny dog. What section is this picture in?

b. Find an illustration showing one pile of books. How many books are there in this pile?

c. What is the title of the poem in the *Pen to paper* section?

d. One of the following pictures is not used in this unit. Which one?

1

Galeria Nacional de Arte, Washington DC. Fotografia: ID/BR

3

Lewis Gillingham/Getty Images

2

Ginny Filer/Shutterstock.com/ID/BR

4

Manny Carabel/Getty Images

Não escreva no livro.

A first approach

Talking about the topic

1. What is the common situation in all these images?
2. There are some famous people represented here. Who are they?
3. What continents are being represented in three of these images?
4. Which of these pictures do you like best? Is it a photo or a painting?

Portrait Images Asia By Nonwarit/Shutterstock.com/ID/BR

Rachel Guedes/Folhapress

Galeria Nacional de Arte, Washington DC. Fotografia: ID/BR

Margaret Bourke-White/Time & Life Pictures/Getty Images

Themba Hadebe/AP Photo/Imageplus

Coleção particular. Fotografia: ID/BR

Não escreva no livro.

Exploring the topic

1. Match the descriptions below to the images on the previous page and write the combinations in your notebook.

A It shows an important South African leader, Nelson Mandela (1918-2013). His story was told in books, documentaries, and in the film *Invictus*.

B It shows a teenager reading a book in a park.

C It shows an important Indian leader, Mahatma Gandhi (1869-1948). His story was told in books, documentaries, and in a very successful movie.

D It shows an important cordel artist, Master Azulão (1932-2016), of what is called "cordel literature".

E It shows *The Mother and Sister of the Artist*, a painting (oil on canvas) by Berthe Morisot (France, 1869/1870. 101 cm × 81,8 cm.).

F It shows *Mornings together*, a painting (oil on canvas) by Daniel Gerhartz (USA, 1965. 30 cm × 30 cm.).

2. This text is related to one of the pictures on the previous page. Test your translation skills. Look at the numbered words below and, in your notebook, complete the text with their equivalent in English. Then, your teacher will read the whole text for you to check your answers.

I expressão	**III** mercados	**V** criar	**VII** tipo
II rua	**IV** normalmente	**VI** personagem	

"Cordel literature" is an important cultural **I** in the Northeast of Brazil. It is named for the way **II** vendors display it at **III**, newsstands, fairs, etc. The pamphlets (*folhetos*) are displayed hanging from a string (see image on the right). "Cordel literature" is **IV** illustrated with woodcuts (xylography). The choice of themes to **V** a *folheto* is unlimited. It can be a regional **VI** as "Lampião", a love story, or important events of public interest. This **VII** of literature is also common in Italy, Spain, Portugal, and Mexico.

J. L. Bulcão/Pulsar Imagens

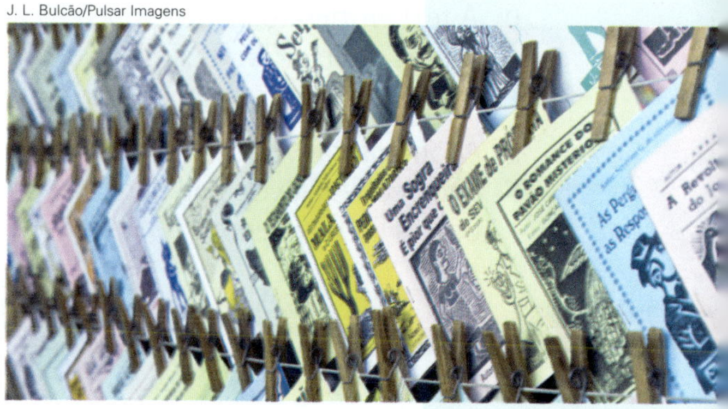

Looking around

1. Is reading a common activity in your family? Who is the most regular reader among your family members or relatives?

2. Pictures on the previous page show people reading. Do you think reading is important? Why (not)?

3. Think about people who can't read. How can they have access to literary texts?

Não escreva no livro.

Reading corner

Pre-reading

1. Look at the picture and talk about these questions to your classmates.
   a. Do you think this place is a library or a bookstore? How do you know?
   b. What can help people find the book they want in this place?
   c. Do you have access to a place like this near your house?

Paul Rapson/Alamy/Fotoarena

2. Read the definitions below and match each one to its corresponding literary genre. Then, write the combinations in your notebook.

A An artistic form of expression that uses beautiful or unusual language arranged in fixed lines that have a particular beat and normally rhyme.

B An informative and factual text that describes the life of a particular person. The verb tense used is frequently the past. The use of photos is also common.

C A traditional children's story usually involving kings and princes, magic powers and good and evil characters. It usually teaches the reader a lesson.

D A text written to be performed by actors in a theater or on the radio or TV. It can be performed by one single actor (monologue) or several actors (dialogues).

E A long narrative about imaginary or partly imaginary events and people. Novels and detective stories are some examples of this literary genre.

Babek Hasanoff/Shutterstock.com/ID/BR

Exploring the text

1. Look at three pieces of writing. Read them quickly and write in your notebook the option that best defines each type of text.

Text 1

All through the night, your glorious eyes
Were gazing down in mine,
And, with a full heart's thankful sighs,
I blessed that watch divine.

Second stanza of "Stars", by Emily Brontë. Available at https://www.poemhunter.com/poem/stars-9. Accessed on March 15, 2022.

Kanate/Shutterstock.com/ID/BR

A biography
B fiction (novel)
C poem
D play
E fairy tale

Não escreva no livro.

Text 2

Kanate/Shutterstock.com/ID/BR

The wretched face of the guard fills my mind as the ghost of his grip burns my thigh. The memory of his glare propels me. I leap into the first boat.

"Zélie, watch out!" Kana cries out, cradling her precious fruit. Our village gardener adjusts her headwrap and scowls as I hop onto a wooden barge teeming with blue moonfish.

"Sorry!"

I yell apology after apology, leaping from boat to boat like a red-nosed frogger. As soon as I land on the deck of the fishermen's sector, I'm off, relishing in the sensation of my feet pounding against the wooden planks. Though Tzain now trails behind, I keep going, I need to reach Baba first. If it's bad, Tzain'll need a warning.

Henry Holt and Co./Arquivo da editora

Tomi Adeyemi. *Children of Blood and Bone*. New York: Henry and Holt Company, 2018. p. 33.

A biography **B** fiction (novel) **C** poem **D** play **E** fairy tale

Text 3

Kanate/Shutterstock.com/ID/BR

A long time ago, in a far-off land, there lived a foolish king who decided that he alone should have the power of magic.

He therefore commanded the head of his army to form a Brigade of Witch-Hunters, and issued them with a pack of ferocious black hounds. At the same time, the King caused proclamations to be read in every village and town across the land: "Wanted by the King, an Instructor in Magic."

No true witch or wizard dared volunteer for the post, for they were all in hiding from the Brigade of Witch-Hunters.

However, a cunning charlatan with no magical power saw a chance of enriching himself, and arrived at the palace, claiming to be a wizard of enormous skill.

Bloomsbury Publication/Arquivo da editora

J. K. Rowling. *The Tales of Beedle the Bard*. London: Bloomsbury Publishing Plc., 2008. p. 63-64.

A biography **B** fiction (novel) **C** poem **D** play **E** fairy tale

2. The three pieces of writing you have read are only fragments of the original texts. Read them carefully now and decide: Is it possible to understand the context of each fragment? Use your notebook to write about what you could understand from each text.

3. Work in groups. Discuss the ideas that each student had while reading the three texts. Use these prompts to talk about what you wrote in activity 2.

IN TEXT 1, THE WRITER IS SAYING THAT...

IN TEXT 2, THE SITUATION INVOLVES...

FROM TEXT 3, I UNDERSTOOD THAT...

Dictionary 23

scowl *verb* UK /skaʊl/ US /skaʊl/

Definition: to look at someone or something with a very annoyed expression.

Available at https://dictionary.cambridge.org/pt/dicionario/ingles/scowl. Accessed on March 15, 2022.

Não escreva no livro.

4. Still in groups, use your notebooks to create a chart similar to the one below and complete it with information from the texts. Write a question mark in the items which you can't find any information about in the text.

Text	Title	Author	Genre	Year of publication	Place of publication	Name of the publisher
1	|||||||||||||||||||	|||||||||||||||||||	|||||||||||||||||||	|||||||||||||||||||	|||||||||||||||||||	|||||||||||||||||||

5. Now, based on the previous activity, answer these questions in your notebook.

a. When was *Children of Blood and Bone* published?

b. Where was *The Tales of Beedle the Bard* published?

c. What kind of text is "Stars"?

d. Was "Stars" written by J. K. Rowling?

e. Did Tomi Adeyemi write a fiction for teenagers?

f. What is Bloomsbury?

6. Read a fragment of an article about one of the authors mentioned in this section and the five statements that follow it. Then, discuss with your classmates if you agree or disagree with those statements.

Author of *Children of Blood and Bone* says her debut novel was a response to genre fiction in which the characters were always white. [...]

But Tomi Adeyemi, the 24-year-old Nigerian-American author of *Children of Blood and Bone*, says that such success was the last thing on her mind when she sat down to write her epic tale of an oppressive world where magic has been outlawed.

"For the past 10 months I've spent a lot of time thinking, is this for real?" she says. "I had a lot of different reasons for writing the book but at its core was the desire to write for black teenage girls growing up reading books they were absent from. That was my experience as a child. *Children of Blood and Bone* is a chance to address that. To say you are seen."

Available at https://www.theguardian.com/books/2018/mar/10/tomi-adeyemi-interview-children-of-blood-and-bone-sarah-hughes. Accessed on March 15, 2022.

Manny Carabel/Getty Images

Tomi Adeyemi.

a. Writing books for teenagers is a money-making business.

b. All teenagers like stories about witches and wizards.

c. All teenagers like to identify themselves with the characters in a story.

d. All authors write what publishers want them to write to make more money.

e. Tomi Adeyemi will never include any more black characters in her books.

Words, words, words

Words related to library

1. In your notebook, do the quiz below to test your English vocabulary skills. Then, in pairs, compare your answers.

A	The word "library" means:	I "biblioteca".	II "livraria".
B	"He is a 'bookworm'" means:	I "Ele é uma 'traça'".	II "Ele é um 'rato de biblioteca'".
C	"Encyclopaedia" is:	I the way British people write "enciclopédia".	II the way Americans write "enciclopédia".
D	"Catalog" is:	I the way Americans write "catálogo".	II the way British people write "catálogo".
E	A "librarian" is a:	I "livreiro".	II "bibliotecário".
F	"To borrow a book" means:	I "pedir um livro emprestado".	II "emprestar um livro".
G	"To lend a book" means:	I "pedir emprestado um livro".	II "emprestar um livro".
H	"Periodical" means:	I "periodicamente".	II "publicação periódica".

2. Some of the English words in activity 1 appear in the next three texts. Find them and make a list in your notebook.

Text 1

A library is a room or a building with a collection of books, periodicals, and other materials. The first libraries were set up in ancient Egypt and Babylon.

In addition to libraries that are open to the public, many important libraries are attached to schools, colleges, and government organizations. The largest library in the world is the Library of Congress in Washington, D.C.

Most libraries work the same way and have the same rules. Users are expected to be quiet and to take good care of the books, periodicals, and other materials. The most important part of any library – apart from the books and other resources – is the librarian. He or she is there to help visitors find the books they need and to guide them through the library system and the catalog.

Scholastic Children's Encyclopedia. New York: Scholastic Inc., 2004. p. 356.

Não escreva no livro.

Text 2

The library of Alexandria is a legend. Not a myth, but a legend.

Library of Alexandria, famous ancient library, considered to have the greatest collection of books in the ancient world. Founded by Ptolemy I Soter, king of Egypt, in the city of Alexandria, it was expanded by his son Ptolemy II Philadelphus early in the 3rd century BC. At its peak it may have preserved 400,000 to 700,000 papyrus scrolls – the largest collection of recorded information in the ancient world.

According to legend, the library at Alexandria was burned at least three times.

Azmie9311/Shutterstock.com/ID/BR

The rebuilding of The Library of Alexandria began in 1995. The new "Bibliotheca Alexandrina" opened to the public in 2002. This photograph was taken in 2017 and shows the entrance of the Egyptian library.

YANCOM/ID/BR

Available at http://www.systemslibrarian.co.za/first-librarian.html. Accessed on March 15, 2022.

Text 3

"Did you know", Mrs. Phelps said, "that public libraries like this allow you to borrow books and take them home?"

"I didn't know that," Matilda said. "Could I do it?"

"Of course," Mrs. Phelps said. "When you have chosen the book you want, bring it to me so I can make a note of it and it's yours for two weeks. You can take more than one if you wish."

Roald Dahl. *Matilda*. New York: Puffin Books, 1996. p. 18-19.

De Fontein/Arquivo da Editora

YANCOM/ID/BR

3. Now, read the three texts more carefully and select four words or expressions that you could not understand. Copy them into your notebook.

4. Talk to your classmates. Can they help you understand the meaning of the items you selected in activity 3? Can you help them understand the meaning of the items they selected?

5. In your notebook, organize a mini glossary including at least ten entries taken from the texts in this section. Look at the examples below.

Word	Noun? Verb? Adjective?	Definition in Portuguese
allow	verb (v)	permitir
book	noun (n)	livro
important	adjective (adj)	importante

6. Suppose you have to post on the web a version in Portuguese of one of the three texts presented here. In your notebook, write a translation of the text you have chosen. Ask your teacher to give you feedback.

Grammar bits

Present perfect

1. Look at the titles of four books. What kind of books do you think they are? Match the titles to the genres and write the combinations in your notebook.

I humor	**III** thriller	**V** science
II biography	**IV** history	**VI** almanac

Henry Holt and Co./Arquivo da editora

A *Blue Latitudes: Boldly Going Where Captain Cook Has Gone Before*

Hodder Children's/Arquivo da editora

C *The Dog's Just Been Sick in the Honda*

B *Nineteen: a Reflection of My Teenage Experience in an Extraordinary Life: What I Have Learned, and What I Have to Share*

Jacquie Jordan Inc. Publishing/Tvguestpert/Arquivo da editora

D *Have you Seen This Face?: the Work of Forensic Artists*

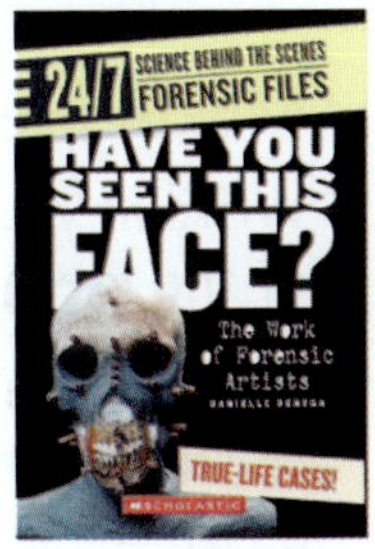

Scholastic/Arquivo da editora

2. Find in the titles above the following verb forms: see / learn / be / go. Copy them into your notebook the way they appear in the titles and answer these questions in your notebook.

a. In the titles, what verb is pairing up with these verb forms?

I be **II** go **III** have

b. Do the four titles refer to the present or to the past? Do they contain any time expressions like *yesterday*, *two years ago*, *in 2016*, etc.?

Making sense

Based on your answers in activity 2, in your notebook, complete these statements about the use of the Present perfect.

a. We use the Present perfect to talk about actions or experiences in the **I**.

b. We always use two verbs: **II** or **III** (3rd person singular) and the past participle of the main verb (*been*, *gone*, *seen*, etc.).

c. If the verb is regular, such as *learn*, we add **IV** in the past and past participle. If the verb is **V** such as *be*, *go*, and *see*, the verb forms are different and there isn't a rule.

d. The Present perfect is used to talk about a general past. That is why we **IV** specific past time expressions.

Não escreva no livro.

3. Read this fragment of the introduction of a book called *Think of a Link*. Then, choose the best answer for you and write it in your notebook.

Have you ever dreamed of remembering absolutely everything in the whole wide world? Every capital city, every date, every king and queen, every meaning of every word, every spelling, and even every type of chocolate bar you've ever heard of?

Andy Salmon. *Think of a Link*: how to Remember Absolutely Everything. London: Scholastic Children's Books, 2011. p. 6.

Bonkers Books/Arquivo da editora

I Yes, I have. **II** No, I haven't.

4. Now, answer in your notebook these questions about yourself.

a. Have you ever read any of the *Harry Potter* books?

b. Have you ever met a book writer in person?

c. Have your parents ever bought any book through the Internet?

Making sense

Write in your notebook the appropriate options to complete these statements about the use of the Present perfect.

a. To form a question, we put the auxiliary verb *have* or *has* **I** (**after** / **before** / **between**) the subject and the main verb.

b. We don't use expressions like *yesterday*, *last night*, *a minute ago*, etc., BUT we use the adverb *ever* **II** (**to ask** / **to answer**) about past experiences.

c. To form the negative, we put *not* after the auxiliary verb. We can also make a contraction. Examples: "They **III** (**not have** / **haven't** / **hasn't**) read this book." / "My little sister **IV** (**not have** / **haven't** / **hasn't**) learned how to read."

5. Read this riddle and copy into your notebook the verb in the Present perfect. Then, tell a classmate what you could understand about the context.

Question: When do we put a saddle on a horse backwards?

Answer: When we want to see the places where we have been.

Illustrations: Claudio Chiyo/ID/BR; Christos Georghiou/Shutterstock.com/ID/BR

6. Read this poem by George Eliot. Then, copy into your notebook the lines with cases of Present perfect.

Count That Day Lost

If you sit down at set of sun
And count the acts that you have done,
And, counting, find
One self-denying deed, one word
That eased the heart of him who heard,
One glance most kind
That fell like sunshine where it went —
Then you may count that day well spent.

But if, through all the livelong day,
You've cheered no heart, by yea or nay —
If, through it all
You've nothing done that you can trace
That brought the sunshine to one face —
No act most small
That helped some soul and nothing cost —
Then count that day as worse than lost.

Available at http://www.poemhunter.com/poem/count-that-day-lost/. Accessed on March 15, 2022.

Quick quiz – Let's talk!

Universal History Archive/Universal Images Group/Getty Images

George Eliot (1819-1880) was the pen name used by a female English writer. She adopted this pseudonym because, at that time, the job of a writer was considered a male job. In other words, only men were respected as writers. Was George Eliot's real name **Louise Evans**, **Mary Ann Evans** or **Margaret Evans**?

Dictionary 24

glance *noun* UK /glɑːns/ US /glæns/
Definition: a quick look at someone or something.

Available at https://dictionary.cambridge.org/dictionary/english/glance. Accessed on May 3, 2022.

7. Based on the poem, would you say your days have been well spent lately? Have you said anything to ease the heart of anybody? Have you brought the sunshine to anybody? Talk about these questions to your classmates.

Discussion point

- No passado, usar um nome masculino garantiu a uma escritora inglesa o reconhecimento de seu trabalho literário. Você acha que a situação hoje em dia é diferente? Quais escritoras você conhece? Elas têm tanto prestígio quanto os escritores?

Go to **Grammar reference** (unit 8).

Open your ears

1. In the text below, an English teacher talks about what happened with two of his six-year-old students during a class. Read it and talk to your classmates about the following questions.

> A few years ago, I was teaching a Year 2 class in East London. We had been working on writing stories. When it came to sharing what they had written, one boy, who had recently arrived from Nigeria, was eager to read his work to the class.
>
> As he read out his protagonist's name – I had suggested that children might use the names of people in their family – another boy, who was born in Britain and identified as Congolese, interrupted him.
>
> "You can't do that! Stories have to be about white people," he said.
>
> Available at http://rapclassroom.blogspot.com/. Accessed on March 15, 2022.

a. Do you agree that "stories have to be about white people"? Why (not)?

b. Why do you think the second boy said that?

c. Have you ever read a story that you identified yourself with the main character? Which one?

2. You are going to listen to part of a TV news report on a topic related to the text above. What other topics do you think the report deals with? Read the options below and write the answer in your notebook.

a. The themes authors in general prefer to explore.

b. Inclusive characters are still insufficiently or inadequately representated in most children's books.

c. A list with some of the most popular children's book titles.

25 **3.** Listen to the recording and check if your predictions in activity 2 were correct.

25 **4.** Listen to the recording again and, in your notebook, complete the text below using the words from the box.

compassion	normal	different
world	children	feel

"I think it's so important that **I** get to see themselves in the books that they read, and that they get to see into the lives of other people who are a bit **II** from them. So... it helps people grow in **III** and respect, it helps them **IV** validated and **V** and understand their place in the **VI**."

5. Think about your own experience as a reader and talk to your classmates: When you read a book, do you like to see yourself in the story? Why (not)?

Speaker's corner

Doing a survey and reporting your findings

1. This questionnaire will make you think about your reading habits. Write in your notebook the most appropriate answers for you or add your own answers.

a. Where do you normally read?

b. When do you usually read?

c. How do you normally read?

d. Do you ever cheat and read the end first?

e. Do you ever read the same book more than once?

f. Do you prefer to read an e-book or a book?

g. Do you read every word or skip some parts?

Ginny Filer/Shutterstock.com/ID/BR

2. Compare your answers to a classmate's. Do you have similar reading habits?

3. You are going to send a contribution to an educational website about the favorite titles in Middle School Literature in Brazil. Do this survey with one classmate and two teachers. If your teachers don't speak English, help them. Remember to explain to the interviewees the objective of this survey.

a. What was the title of a book that you had to read for school and that you liked?

b. What kind of book was it? (Juvenile fiction? Thriller? Humor?)

c. What was interesting about it? (Plot? Characters? Theme? Author's style?)

d. Have you read it again?

4. Write in your notebook the sentences you may use to talk about your findings.

I The book most people mentioned was...

II Most people read... (juvenile fiction/thriller/humor/etc.) books.

III Most people have said that the... (plot/characters/theme/author's style) was/were really interesting.

IV Only one person has (or Two people have) read the book again.

Pen to paper

Writing a stanza of a poem

Pre-writing

1. Look back at the two poems in this unit, one in the *Reading corner* section and the other in the *Grammar bits* section. Then, think: What makes people write poems? Natural talent? Happiness? Frustration? Look at these images and choose from the following options some possible situations that can inspire writers.

Picton/Shutterstock.com/ID/BR

Rawpixel.com/Shutterstock.com/ID/BR

4 PM production/Shutterstock.com/ID/BR

Creative Travel Projects/ Shutterstock.com/ID/BR

I the ocean
II nature
III animals
IV flowers
V family
VI children
VII love
VIII friends

2. Read the three first stanzas of another poem written by George Eliot (Mary Ann Evans). What seems to be the biggest inspiration for the author: the greatness of the world or the absence of her sister?

The world is great

The world is great!
The birds fly from me;
The stars are golden fruit
Upon a tree
All out of reach
My little sister went and I am lonely.

The world is great!
I tried to mount the hill
Above the pines
Where the light lies so still,
But it rose higher.
Little Lisa went and I am lonely.

The world is great!
The wind comes rushing by.
I wonder where it comes from.
Sea-birds cry
And hurt my heart.
My little sister went and I am lonely.

YANCOM/ID/BR

Available at http://www.poemhunter.com/poem/the-world-is-great/. Accessed on March 15, 2022.

Não escreva no livro.

Follow these steps to write the last stanza of the poem on page 126

1. Observe the poem again and answer these questions in your notebook.

   a. Are there rhyming words?

   b. How many verses are there in each stanza?

   c. Are the verses very long or short?

   d. Are there verses that repeat in the poem?

2. You are going to write the last stanza of the poem "The world is great". Consider the following items:

   a. In general, it is not a rule to include rhyming words, but in the case of this poem, it is very important to do it. Read the poem out loud to confirm.

   b. In general, it is not a rule to repeat a verse in the beginning of each stanza, but in this case it is also very important.

3. Pay attention to the type of language used in the poem. Write in your notebook what you can observe.

   I Only the Simple present is used.

   II The Simple past and the Simple present are used.

   III Adjectives are used in all the stanzas.

   IV The interrogative form is used.

   V The rhyming words are always in lines 2 and 4 of each stanza.

4. In your notebook, write a first draft of the stanza. Think about a possible scenario for the poem.

5. Exchange your first draft with some classmates. Ask them to comment on what you wrote and to give suggestions. Write another version considering your classmates' ideas. Give it to your teacher for feedback.

6. Write one more version of the text, now considering your teacher's comments and the evaluation below. Use your notebook.

Evaluate yourself

1. Releia sua estrofe e responda no caderno:

   a. O tamanho da estrofe que produzi está compatível com o tamanho das demais estrofes?

   b. Iniciei o primeiro verso da mesma maneira que a autora?

   c. Mencionei a *little sister* no último verso?

   d. Usei as rimas adequadamente, conforme ocorre nas demais estrofes?

2. Decida se é preciso reescrever sua estrofe e faça as correções necessárias.

3. Organize com os colegas um livro de poesias com as diferentes versões do poema "The world is great". O título do livro pode ser *One poem... different endings*.

Não escreva no livro.

Focus on culture

Spoken literature

How Shakespeare influences the way we speak now

During his 52 years on earth, William Shakespeare enriched the English language in ways so profound it's almost impossible to fully gauge his impact. Without him, our vocabulary would be just too different. He gave us uniquely vivid ways in which to express hope and despair, sorrow and rage, love and lust. Even if you've never read one of his sonnets or seen a play – even if you've never so much as watched a movie adaptation – you're likely to have quoted him unwittingly. [...]

If you've ever been 'in a pickle', waited 'with bated breath', or gone on 'a wild goose chase', you've been quoting from *The Tempest*, *The Merchant of Venice* and *Romeo and Juliet* respectively.

Next time you refer to jealousy as "the green-eyed monster," know that you're quoting Othello's arch villain, Iago. Allow yourself to "gossip" (*A Midsummer Night's Dream*), and you're quoting him. [...]

Galeria Nacional de Retratos, Londres. Fotografia: ID/BR

His impact endures not only in the way we express ourselves, but how we experience and process the world around us. [...]

If the mark of a great writer is that they're still read, then perhaps the mark of a genius is that they're still spoken, too.

Available at https://www.bbc.com/culture/story/20140527-say-what-shakespeares-words. Accessed on March 15, 2022.

1. Read the text with attention and, then, talk to your classmates about these questions.

a. How many Shakespeare's plays can you name?

b. Have you ever seen a movie, a play, or a soap opera based on a Shakespeare's play? Which was it?

c. What other English writers do you know?

d. What was the last book you read? Why did you choose that book? How did you like it?

2. Do some research about authors that influence their countries and culture. Choose one author and create a poster about his/her life and work. Then, show it to your classmates.

Self-assessment

Reflect about your own learning

assessment · learning · reflect · autonomy · English · responsibility · feedback

Freepik/ID/BR

I do it with confidence.	I do it well.	I can get better.

1. Como você avalia seu aprendizado nesta unidade? Reflita.

a. Que parte da unidade (seção, texto, imagem, mensagem do tutor, etc.) mais lhe agradou? Por quê?

b. Qual foi a parte de que você menos gostou? Por quê?

c. Você se lembra de alguma coisa que viu nesta unidade e que o ajudou fora da aula de inglês?

2. O que você pode fazer para melhorar seu aprendizado de inglês? Observe as opções abaixo e pense a respeito delas.

- Ler mais.
- Fazer mais atividades.
- Solucionar dúvidas com o professor.
- Trocar ideias com os colegas.
- Ouvir músicas em inglês.
- Assistir a filmes em inglês com legendas.

Cookie Studio/Shutterstock.com/ID/BR

Não escreva no livro.

Grammar reference

Unit 1

Passive voice (Simple past)

It is formed by the verb *to be* in the Simple past + the past participle of the main verb.

*The word "television" **was used** for the first time in 1900.*

*A machine called Pantelegraph **was invented** in 1862.*

*Cable television systems **were introduced** in Pennsylvania and Oregon.*

If you know who or what did the action and if you think it is relevant to mention this information, you place the agent at the end of the sentence, preceded by the word **by**.

*The first moving silhouette images **were created** by John Baird.*

*The first color TV program **was broadcast** by CBS.*

*Black and white broadcasting experiments **were conducted** by RCA.*

Comparative adjectives

We use the comparative to compare two things or people.

If the adjective is short (one or two syllables), we add **–er** to the end of it.
Pay attention to spelling.

old	old**er** (than)
nice	nice**r** (than)
big	big**ger** (than)
hard	hard**er** (than)
cheap	cheap**er** (than)

If the adjective is short (one or two syllables), but finishes in **–y**, we change the end to **–ier**.
Pay attention to spelling.

happy	happ**ier** (than)
angry	angr**ier** (than)
hungry	hungr**ier** (than)
busy	bus**ier** (than)
dirty	dirt**ier** (than)

If the adjective is long (three or more syllables), we use the word **more** before it.

interesting	**more** interesting (than)
beautiful	**more** beautiful (than)
important	**more** important (than)
comfortable	**more** comfortable (than)
exciting	**more** exciting (than)

Remember these important exceptions:

good	**better** (than)
bad	**worse** (than)
far	**further** (than)

Unit 2

Relative pronouns

	Used for...	Example
who	people	A chef is someone **who** cooks in a restaurant. Cleaner is someone **who** cleans somewhere.
which	things	A knife is an object **which** cuts things. A sponge is an object **which** washes things.
that	people/things	A chef is someone **that** cooks in a restaurant. Cleaner is someone **that** cleans somewhere. A knife is an object **that** cuts things. A sponge is an object **that** washes things.
whose	possessions	**Whose** pencil is this? **Whose** history is this?

Superlative adjectives

We use the superlative to compare one thing or person to two or more other things or people.

If the adjective is short (one or two syllables), we add **–est** to the end of it. We always use the word **the** before the superlative adjective. Pay attention to spelling.

old	the old**est**
nice	the nic**est**
big	the bigg**est**
hard	the hard**est**
cheap	the cheap**est**

If the adjective is short (one or two syllables), but finishes in **–y**, we change the end to **–iest**. We also always use the word **the** before it. Pay attention to spelling.

happy	the happ**iest**
angry	the angr**iest**
hungry	the hungr**iest**
busy	the bus**iest**
dirty	the dirt**iest**

If the adjective is long (three or more syllables), we use **the most** before it.

interesting	**the most** interesting
beautiful	**the most** beautiful
important	**the most** important
comfortable	**the most** comfortable
exciting	**the most** exciting

Remember these important exceptions:

good	**the best**
bad	**the worst**
far	**the further**

Unit 3

Modal verbs

Modal verb	To express...	Example
can	ability	I **can** read in Spanish. She **can** play the bass.
have to must	obligation	You **have to** follow rules at school. He **has to** follow rules at the game. We **must** get permission from our parents.
can may might could	possibility	You **can** count on me. You **may** find a way to help poor people. He **might** find something he likes to do. You **could** meet new people working as a volunteer.
should	advice	You **should** be more active. You **shouldn't** watch so much TV.

Unit 4

Countable and uncountable nouns

Countable nouns are those that we use to refer to something that **can be counted**. Those nouns can be used in **singular** and **plural** forms.

	Countable nouns
Examples	egg/eggs, carrot/carrots, apple/apples, date/dates
Expressions	(not) many, few, a few, some, any

Uncountable nouns are those that we use to refer to something that **can't be counted**. Those nouns can be used only in **singular** form.

	Uncountable nouns
Examples	water, vegetable oil, flour, sugar
Expressions	(not) much, little, a little, some, any

Attention

- We use **how many** when we have to ask about **countable** things.
  How many apples would we need?
  How many eggs do you use for this recipe?
- We use **how much** when we have to ask about **uncountable** things.
  How much sugar did you buy?
  How much water do we use for this recipe?

Any/some

In general, we use **any** in **negative** and **interrogative** sentences.

*I don't need **any** water.*

*Do you want **any** carrots?*

*Do I need to buy **any** oranges for this recipe?*

However, we can use ***some*** for ***interrogative*** sentences too, but only when we expect the answer will be positive.

*Do you need **some** help? **Yes**, please!*

*Do you want **some** cake, Melissa? **Yes**, I want **some** cake, please!*

We use ***some*** also for affirmative sentences.

*Do you want **any** carrots? Yes, I want **some** carrots to do a cake.*

*Do I need to buy **any** oranges for this recipe? Yes, you need **some** oranges to do the juice.*

Unit 5

There is / There are / There was / There were

We use **There is** / **There are** to talk about existence in the present.

Affirmative	Negative	Interrogative
There is a computer in the classroom.	**There isn't (is not)** a computer in the classroom.	**Is there** a computer in the classroom?
There are five computers in the lab.	**There aren't (are not)** five computers in the lab.	**Are there** five computers in the lab?

We use **There was** / **There were** to talk about existence in the past.

Affirmative	Negative	Interrogative
There was a television in this room.	**There wasn't (was not)** a television in this room.	**Was there** a television in this room?
There were two televisions in this room.	**There weren't (were not)** two televisions in this room.	**Were there** two televisions in this room?

Short answers (Present)			
Singular		Plural	
Yes,	there is.	Yes,	there are.
No,	there isn't.	No,	there aren't.

Short answers (Past)			
Singular		Plural	
Yes,	there was.	Yes,	there were.
No,	there wasn't.	No,	there weren't.

Used to

We use **used to** to talk about habits that we don't have anymore.

Affirmative	Negative	Interrogative
My grandfather **used to** listen to football games on the radio.	My grandfather **didn't use to** listen to football games on the radio.	**Did** my grandfather **use to** listen to football games on the radio?

Unit 6

Question words

To ask about...	
what	... things **What** is the biggest country in the world?
who	... people **Who** is the most famous soccer player in the world?
where	... places **Where** can I find a cybercafe in this neighborhood?
when	... time **When** was the last time you went to the beach?
how	... manner **How** do Brazilians usually celebrate Christmas?
why	... reasons **Why** are you so happy today?

Unit 7

Future with *will*

We use **will** to talk about something we decided to do at the time of speaking and to express expectations and opinions about the future.

Form: subject (I/You/He/She/It/We/You/They) + *will* + main verb + complement

Affirmative	Negative	Interrogative
I **will** / **'ll** see her again by the end of the year.	I **will not** / **won't** see her again by the end of the year.	**Will** I see her again by the end of the year?
You **will** / **'ll** meet him in front of the market in half an hour.	You **will not** / **won't** meet him in front of the market in half an hour.	**Will** you meet him in front of the market in half an hour?
He **will** / **'ll** teach Peter how to use the computer.	He **will not** / **won't** teach Peter how to use the computer.	**Will** he teach Peter how to use the computer?
She **will** / **'ll** tell Jonas what happened.	She **will not** / **won't** tell Jonas what happened.	**Will** she tell Jonas what happened?
We **will** / **'ll** pass the exam easily.	We **will not** / **won't** pass the exam easily.	**Will** we pass the exam easily?
They **will** / **'ll** be in England by next January.	They **will not** / **won't** be in England by next January.	**Will** they be in England by next January?

Short answers					
Affirmative			**Negative**		
Yes,	I	will.	No,	I	won't.
	you			you	
	he/she/it			he/she/it	
	we/you/they			we/you/they	

Future with *going to*

We use **going to** to talk about decisions and plans.

Form: subject (I/You/He/She/It/We/You/They) + present of *to be* (am/is/are) + *going to* + main verb + + complement

Affirmative	Negative	Interrogative
I **am going to study** more.	I **'m (not) going to study** more.	**Am I going to study** more?
You **are going to play** tennis.	You **aren't (are not) going to play** tennis.	**Are** you **going to play** tennis?
He **is going to eat** healthy food.	He **isn't (is not) going to eat** healthy food.	**Is** he **going to eat** healthy food?
She **is going to read** a book.	She **isn't (is not) going to read** a book.	**Is** she **going to read** a book?
We **are going to watch** a movie.	We **aren't (are not) going to watch** a movie.	**Are** we **going to watch** a movie?
You **are going to buy** a shirt.	You **aren't (are not) going to buy** a shirt.	**Are** you **going to buy** a shirt?
They **are going to travel**.	They **aren't (are not) going to travel**.	**Are** they **going to travel**?

Attention

- We use (**be**) **going to** when we have already decided to do something.
  We're going to movies on Saturday.
- We use **will** when we decide to do something at the time of speaking.
  I didn't know she was not feeling well. I'll go and visit her.
- Imagine this situation: you got involved in an accident which caused serious damage to your bicycle. A friends asks what you are planning to do about the bicycle. If you don't know what to do yet, but you're thinking about selling it, you can say:
  I don't know yet. I think I'll sell it.
  But, if you have decided what to do, you can say:
  It's too expensive to repair my bike. I'm going to sell it.

Não escreva no livro.

Unit 8

Present perfect

Affirmative (*long and short form*)	Negative (*long and short form*)	Interrogative
I **have read** this book. I**'ve read** this book.	I **have not read** this book. I **haven't read** this book.	**Have** you **read** this book?
You **have told** me the story. You**'ve told** me the story.	You **have not told** me the story. You **haven't told** me the story.	**Have** you **told** me the story?
He **has bought** this CD through the Internet. He**'s bought** this CD through the Internet.	He **has not bought** this CD through the Internet. He **hasn't bought** this CD through the Internet.	**Has** he **bought** this CD through the Internet?
She **has met** that famous writer. She**'s met** that famous writer.	She **has not met** that famous writer. She**'s not met** that famous writer.	**Has** she **met** that famous writer?
It **has arrived**. It**'s arrived**.	It **has not arrived**. It **hasn't arrived**.	**Has** it **arrived**?
We **have been** there. We**'ve been** there.	We **have not been** there. We **haven't been** there.	**Have** we **been** there?
You **have learned** English. You**'ve learned** English.	You **have not learned** English. You **haven't learned** English.	**Have** you **learned** English?
They **have borrowed** the books. They**'ve borrowed** the books.	They **have not borrowed** the books. They **haven't borrowed** the books.	**Have** they **borrowed** the books?

Short answers					
Affirmative			Negative		
Yes,	I	have.	No,	I	haven't.
	you			you	
	he/she/it	has.		he/she/it	hasn't.
	we/you/they	have.		we/you/they	haven't.

Attention

- We use the Present perfect to talk about actions or experiences in the past, but if we want to specify when something happened, we use the Simple past and an appropriate time expression.
  I've read this book. (Present perfect) / *I read it last year.* (Simple past)
- We form the Present perfect with **have** or **has** and the past participle of the main verb. The past participle of regular verbs ends in **-ed**, just like the Simple past. Irregular verbs have different forms.
- We use **have been** (and not *have gone*) to talk about places we have visited.
  Have you ever **been** to Argentina? No, I **haven't been** there.

Transcrições de áudio

UNIT 1 ENTERTAINMENT

Faixa 1

Página 12

Listen to the different pronunciations. Repeat the words.

British English: broadcasting, broadcasting

American English: broadcasting, broadcasting

Now listen to the way these people read the same sentence. Pay attention to the differences.

British English: Black and white broadcasting experiments were conducted by RCA.

American English: Black and white broadcasting experiments were conducted by RCA.

Faixa 2

Página 18

It was one of the best scripts I've read in a long time.

[That I] actually as I was reading, I was laughing, and I was crying, and I was stopping to think. Thinking about questioning things I have done and I'm doing as a father, just as a person in society.

And there's so much, so much to discuss and one of the things that really works in the movie is... it comes out its earnestness, that the sense of humor the movie has of not taking itself too seriously, you know. In the beginning it seems it really is going to and then you realize, oh no, it's
an all different thing.

Fonte: Getty Images Entertainment Video/Getty Images

Faixa 3

Página 20

Listen to the different pronunciations of the same word. Repeat after the recording.

British English: eccentric, eccentric

American English: eccentric, eccentric

Now listen to the way these people read the same sentence. Pay attention to the differences.

British English: She was an elderly eccentric who lived with 25 cats.

American English: She was an elderly eccentric who lived with 25 cats.

UNIT 2 FAMOUS PEOPLE

Faixa 4

Página 27

Listen to the different pronunciations of the same word. Repeat after the recording.

British English: spawn, spawn

American English: spawn, spawn

Now listen to the way these people read the same sentence. Pay attention to the differences.

British English: The vague wording of the law has spawned numerous interpretations.

American English: The vague wording of the law has spawned numerous interpretations.

Faixa 5

Página 33

What do you wanna be when you're older?

When you're big and a little bit bolder

What do you want to be?

Maybe you wanna be a firefighter,

Maybe you wanna be a writer,

Just believe in yourself, oh yeah yeah!

Maybe you wanna be a dentist or a doctor

Maybe you wanna be a chemist or a punk rocker

Maybe you wanna be a diplomat or teacher

Claudio Chiyo/ID/BR

Não escreva no livro.

Maybe you wanna be a police man or public speaker, yeah!
What do you wanna be when you're older?
When you're wise and a little bit bolder
What do you want to be?
Maybe you wanna be a nurse,
Maybe you wanna drive a hearse
Just believe in yourself, oh yeah yeah!
Maybe you wanna be an engineer or pilot
Maybe you wanna be an actor, just go on and try it!
Maybe you wanna be a waiter or a banker
Maybe you wanna be a soccer player or news anchor.
Maybe you wanna build some really cool robots
Maybe you wanna be in space just like the astronauts
Maybe you wanna play computer games all day,
Just don't forget to get some exercise and watch your weight.
Maybe you wanna be a lawyer or a judge
Maybe you wanna make some goodies like this chocolate fudge!
What do you wanna be when you're older?
When you're big and a little bit bolder
What do you want to be?

Disponível em: https://www.youtube.com/watch?v=MdvTIQzsaYI. Acesso em: 15 mar. 2022.

Faixa 6

Página 33

Listen to the different pronunciations. Repeat the words.

British English: firefighter, firefighter

Claudio Chiyo/ID/BR

American English: firefighter, firefighter

Now listen to the way these people read the same sentence. Pay attention to the differences.

British English: A firefighter is a person whose job is to stop fires from burning.

American English: A firefighter is a person whose job is to stop fires from burning.

UNIT 3 PEOPLE WHO MAKE A DIFFERENCE

Faixa 7

Página 42

Listen to the different pronunciations. Repeat the words.

British English: volunteer, volunteer

American English: volunteer, volunteer

Now listen to the way these people read the same sentence. Pay attention to the differences.

British English: My brother worked as a volunteer doctor in war zones for two years.

American English: My brother worked as a volunteer doctor in war zones for two years.

Faixa 8

Página 46

Listen to the different pronunciations of the same word. Repeat after the recording.

British English: stir, stir

American English: stir, stir

Now listen to the way these people read the same sentence. Pay attention to the differences.

British English: The alarm clock went off, but she didn't stir.

American English: The alarm clock went off, but she didn't stir.

Faixa 9

Página 47

You've got a friend in me
You've got a friend in me
When the road looks rough ahead
And you're miles and miles
From your nice warm bed

Não escreva no livro.

You just remember what your old pal said
Boy, you've got a friend in me
Yeah, you've got a friend in me

You've got a friend in me
You've got a friend in me
You've got troubles, I've got 'em too
There isn't anything I wouldn't do for you
We stick together and we see it through
Cause you've got a friend in me
You've got a friend in me

Some other folks might be
A little bit smarter than I am
Bigger and stronger too
Maybe
But none of them will ever love you
The way I do
It's me and you, boy

And as the years go by
Our friendship will never die
You're gonna see it's our destiny
You've got a friend in me
You've got a friend in me
You've got a friend in me

Disponível em: https://www.youtube.com/watch?v=DNZUKm0ApEM. Acesso em: 5 maio 2022.

UNIT 4 HEALTH

Faixa 10

Página 55

Listen to the different pronunciations of the same word. Repeat after the recording.

British English: suitable, suitable

American English: suitable, suitable

Now listen to the way these people read the same sentence. Pay attention to the differences.

British English: Each room has books, toys, and games that are suitable to that particular age group.

American English: Each room has books, toys, and games that are suitable to that particular age group.

Faixa 11

Página 60

Listen to the different pronunciations. Repeat the words.

British English: caster sugar, caster sugar

American English: caster sugar, caster sugar

Now listen to the way these people read the same sentence. Pay attention to the differences.

British English: My dad uses caster sugar to cook pancakes.

American English: My dad uses caster sugar to cook pancakes.

Faixa 12

Página 62

Reporter: At the cutting edge of the fight against fat, in the playground of this Junior School in Helsinki, the temperature is subzero, but no one's allowed to sit around inside. In Finland, too, children would instinctively choose what's bad for them. The solution here seems to be to tell them what they've got to have, whether it'll be the food on their plate or how much exercise they must take. School lunches are free and compulsory for all the ten-year-old in this class. Snacks like crisps and chocolate are banned. The same menu for everyone, today pork curry, rice and salad. If you can choose between salad and chips? Chips or hamburgers? Which would you like?

Claudio Chiyo/ID/BR

Não escreva no livro.

Children: Salad.

Reporter: You like salad best.

Children: Yeah.

Reporter: There's skimmed milk to drink, and if you're still hungry, crisp bread and low-fat spread. It's all eaten at their desks. The teacher's reeducating their palates, removing high fat food from the equation.

Teacher: I think children know that that is not an option. We never talk about hamburgers, or this sort of things, or pizza, or something like that... rubbish food or whatever you call it in England.

Fonte: Getty Images/ITN

UNIT 5 TECHNOLOGY

Faixa 13

Página 72

Listen to the different pronunciations. Repeat the words.

British English: self-explanatory, self-explanatory

American English: self-explanatory, self-explanatory

Now listen to the way these people read the same sentence. Pay attention to the differences.

British English: The pictures are self-explanatory.

American English: The pictures are self-explanatory.

Claudio Chiyo/ID/BR

Faixa 14

Página 73

Listen to the different pronunciations of the same word. Repeat after the recording.

British English: gizmo, gizmo

American English: gizmo, gizmo

Now listen to the way these people read the same sentence. Pay attention to the differences.

British English: The store is full of gizmos like pagers and cellular telephones.

American English: The store is full of gizmos like pagers and cellular telephones.

Faixa 15

Página 77

Narrator: How to make a friend in four simple steps. [...]

Step one. Make a list of the things you like to do. Activities, hobbies, interests, write 'em all down and then... Samantha,
I didn't know you like to paint.

Samantha: Yeah, acrylics mostly. [...]

Narrator: Pick out the activities that can be done in group settings.

Step two, do those things. Doing stuff you're into is a surefire way to meet people you already have things in common with. [...]

Step three. Make small talk. I know it sucks, but it's a necessary evil. You might not hit it off with everyone you talk to. But trying is the only way to find someone you do connect with. And now as you're getting to know them, you're probably going to ask the usual...

Samantha: So what do you do? Where are you from?

Narrator: But I recommend something like...

Samantha: So what's been the best part of your week?

Narrator: This can spark more interesting conversation and elevate the small talk to regular size. Just remember to play it by ear. You don't wanna move too fast.

Samantha: I like you. Let's be friends.

Narrator: But don't play it too cool either.

Samantha's friend: We should hang out sometime.

Samantha: Yeah, maybe when my schedule clears up.

Narrator: Basically, just be yourself. You've been subconsciously collecting good friend data your whole life. So if something feels right, give it a shot. Which brings us to step four.

Be a great friend. Making new friends can be intimidating. But what's on the other side is worth the effort. Just remember that friendships aren't found, they're formed. So be patient, present, and the kind of friend you want to have. So do nice things every once in a while. Like giving them your last piece of gum. Unless of course, you need it more.

It may seem weird, but it's these little moments that define true friendship.

When you can look at each other and say, you have some stuff on your face. And not feel awkward. That's when you know it runs deep.

So good job, Samantha. You did it. I hope this helps. [...]

Disponível em: https://www.youtube.com/watch?v=nBWbALQIqlk. Acesso em: 10 mar. 2022.

Claudio Chiyo/ID/BR

UNIT 6 SPECIAL DAYS

Faixa 16

Página 83

Listen to the different pronunciations. Repeat the words.

British English: costume, costume

American English: costume, costume

Now listen to the way these people read the same sentence. Pay attention to the differences.

British English: To celebrate this, people normally wear colorful costumes and dance a lot in the streets.

American English: To celebrate this, people normally wear colorful costumes and dance a lot in the streets.

Faixa 17

Página 85

Listen to the different pronunciations of the same word. Repeat after the recording.

British English: rocking chair, rocking chair

American English: rocking chair, rocking chair

Now listen to the way these people read the same sentence. Pay attention to the differences.

British English: She finds him reading a book in a rocking chair, his back toward her.

American English: She finds him reading a book in a rocking chair, his back toward her.

Faixa 18

Página 90

No New Year's Day to celebrate
No chocolate covered candy hearts to give away
No first of spring
No song to sing
In fact here's just another ordinary day
No April rain
No flowers bloom
No wedding Saturday within the month of June
But what it is, is something true
Made up of these three words that I must say to you
I just called to say I love you
I just called to say how much I care
I just called to say I love you
And I mean it from the bottom of my heart
No summer's high
No warm July
No harvest moon to light one tender August night
No autumn breeze
No falling leaves

Not even time for birds to fly to southern skies
No Libra sun
No Halloween
No giving thanks to all the Christmas joy you bring
But what it is, though old so new
To fill your heart like no three words could ever do

Disponível em: https://www.letras.mus.br/stevie-wonder/43172/. Acesso em: 15 mar. 2022.

UNIT 7 CHANGES

Faixa 19

Página 99

Listen to the different pronunciations. Repeat the words.

British English: scarf, scarf

American English: scarf, scarf

Now listen to the way these people read the same sentence. Pay attention to the differences.

British English: It was cold outside, so Katie put on a scarf.

American English: It was cold outside, so Katie put on a scarf.

Claudio Chiyo/ID/BR

Faixa 20

Página 103

Boy: Dad, can I go outside to play?

Dad: Well, did you get your Saturday's work done?

Boy: Oh, Dad, do I have to?

Dad: Well, you know the rules. No play until the work is done.

Boy: So, what is my work?

Dad: Well, first you have to clean the bathroom, including the toilet. And don't forget to scrub the bathtub.

Boy: No, I want to do the family room.

Dad: Well, OK, but you have to vacuum the family room and the hall, and be sure to dust everything. Oh, and don't forget to wipe the walls and clean the baseboard.

Boy: OK.

Dad: And after that...

Boy: Oh, no!

Dad: Next, sweep and mop the kitchen floor and be sure to polish the table in the living room.

Boy: OK, OK!

Dad: And make your bed and pick up all your toys and put them away. And...

Boy: More?

Dad: Yeah. And then, how about going out for lunch and getting a big milk shake? But, yeah, you probably don't want to do that.

Boy: No, no. I want to.

Dad: OK. While you're doing your work, I'll be out in the yard raking leaves and pulling weeds.

Disponível em: https://www.esl-lab.com/easy/household-chores/. Acesso em: 10 mar. 2022.

Faixa 21

Página 104

Fall is here, hear the yell
Back to school, ring the bell
Brand new shoes, walking blues
Climb the fence, books and pens
I can tell that we are gonna be friends
I can tell that we are gonna be friends

Não escreva no livro.

Walk with me, Suzy Lee
Through the park and by the tree
We will rest upon the ground
And look at all the bugs we found
Safely walk to school without a sound
Safely walk to school without a sound

Here we are, no one else
We walked to school all by ourselves
There's dirt on our uniforms
From chasing all the ants and worms
We clean up and now it's time to learn
We clean up and now it's time to learn

Numbers, letters, learn to spell
Nouns, and books, and show and tell
Playtime we will throw the ball
Back to class, through the hall
Teacher marks our height against the wall
Teacher marks our height against the wall

We don't notice any time pass
We don't notice anything
We sit side by side in every class
Teacher thinks that I sound funny
But she likes the way you sing

Tonight I'll dream while I'm in bed
When silly thoughts go through my head
About the bugs and alphabet
And when I wake tomorrow I'll bet
That you and I will walk together again
I can tell that we are gonna be friends
I can tell that we are gonna be friends.

Disponível em: https://genius.com/The-white-stripes-were-going-to-be-friends-lyrics. Acesso em: 10 mar. 2022.

Faixa 22

Página 107

When you go to High School it can be very overwhelming because there are a lot of students, the school can be a lot bigger than your Middle School and it can be hard to be yourself.

It does, however, make it easier to make friends, believe it or not. Once you make friends you can actually be yourself.

Once you do make friends, however, I do suggest that you'd be careful what you tell your friends. How do you think people find out your business? It's because your friends tell other people.

And it's not that your friends are intentionally trying to do this, it's just gossiping is the big thing in school. So try to be selective of who you tell your business and remember who you tell because if you hear a rumor or that someone else knows then you just know you can't trust that friend.

And you don't want to be that friend that tells other people your friends' business either.

Please try to remember that not everyone you meet is your friend just because they're nice to you.

Just because someone's nice to you or helps you out in some way it doesn't make them your friends. You have to get to know them. I personally do not like when people call me their friend after I just hung out

Claudio Chiyo/ID/BR

Não escreva no livro.

with them one time. How do they know that I even like to hang out with them? And same for me, what if they didn't even like hanging out with me? So, try not to call people your friends unless you've actually shared moments and are hanging out for a while and you feel like you can trust them.

Another thing you should know is that it is possible for your friend to become your enemy and vice versa. You can hate someone one day and then the next day you guys are best friends.

Another thing that I want to mention is do not be that person who make someone stop being friends with someone else just because you don't like that. It happens a lot. Please do not be this person.

Don't make someone stop being someone else's friend just because you don't like that person. You know, it's hard –
I get it – but just try not to be that person because it sucks when you're on the other end.

Disponível em: https://www.youtube.com/watch?v=lqz-GP8KEqQ. Acesso em: 10 mar. 2022.

UNIT 8 LITERATURE FOR LIFE

Faixa 23

Página 117

Listen to the different pronunciations. Repeat the words.

British English: scowl, scowl

American English: scowl, scowl

Now listen to the way these people read the same sentence. Pay attention to the differences.

British English: Everytime I ask something to her, she scowls.

American English: Everytime I ask something to her, she scowls.

Faixa 24

Página 123

Listen to the different pronunciations of the same word. Repeat after the recording.

British English: glance, glance

American English: glance, glance

Now listen to the way these people read the same sentence. Pay attention to the differences.

British English: The driver gave a glance back as he moved into the passing lane.

American English: The driver gave a glance back as he moved into the passing lane.

Faixa 25

Página 124

Lynsey Pollard has recently started a new business packing up books in gifts and posting them to families. The difference is: all the books are inclusive.

"I think it's so important that children get to see themselves in the books that they read, and that they get to see into the lives of other people who are a bit different from them. So... it helps people grow in compassion and respect, it helps them feel validated and normal and understand their place in the world. So I think that is probably one of the most important things you can do. And at the moment we are doing the children a huge disservice by not providing them with the right writing into books so they can see all of the people who are kind of, you know, the society."

Fonte: ITN/Getty Images

Claudio Chiyo/ID/BR

Não escreva no livro.

Glossary

Word list

noun (n) substantivo
adjective (adj) adjetivo
verb (v) verbo
(phr v) phrasal verb
adverb (adv) advérbio
preposition (prep) preposição
interjection (interj) interjeição

A

accent (n) sotaque
achievement (n) realização
action (n) ação

Shahphoto/Shutterstock.com/ID/BR

The students from community promote **actions** for the good of the neighborhood.

actor (n) ator
actress (n) atriz
adolescence (n) adolescência
adventure (n) aventura
afraid (adj) amedrontado(a)
airplane (n) avião
amazing (adj) maravilhoso(a), surpreendente
ankle (n) tornozelo
arm (n) braço
arrive (v) chegar
athlete (n) atleta
autumn (n) outono

B

back (n) costas
backache (n) dor nas costas
bad (adj) mau, má
badly-trained (adj) mal treinado(a)
balanced (adj) balanceado(a), equilibrado(a)
bathroom (n) banheiro
beach (n) praia
bean (n) feijão
beautiful (adj) bonito(a)
bedroom (n) dormitório
bicycle (n) bicicleta
big (adj) grande
bike (n) bicicleta
birth (n) nascimento
birthday (n) aniversário
boat (n) barco
boot up (phr v) inicializar (o computador)

JaysonPhotography/Shutterstock.com/ID/BR

If your computer shows a blue screen, it's to **boot** it **up**.

brain (n) cérebro
bread (n) pão
brush (v) escovar
bus (n) ônibus
bus driver (n) motorista de ônibus

C

camera (n) câmera
camera operator (n) operador(a) de câmera
car (n) carro
carb (n) carboidrato
carbohydrate (n) carboidrato
card (n) cartão
cardiologist (n) cardiologista
careful (adj) cuidadoso(a)
carnival (n) carnaval
carol (n) canção natalina
carpenter (n) marceneiro(a)
cart (n) carroça
cartoon (n) desenho animado
charity (n) instituição de caridade
cheek (n) bochecha
chef (n) chefe de cozinha
chest (n) peito
chicken (n) frango
childhood (n) infância
chin (n) queixo
Christmas (n) Natal
citizen (n) cidadã(o)
climb (v) escalar
coach (n) treinador(a), técnico(a)
cold (adj) frio(a)
comedy (n) comédia
community (n) comunidade
computer systems analyst (n) analista de sistemas
conceited (adj) convencido(a), vaidoso(a)
conductor (n) maestro, maestrina
considerate (adj) atencioso(a)
cooking program (n) programa culinário de TV
cooperative (adj) cooperativo(a)
cow (n) vaca
cunning (adj) esperto

Michele Aldeghi/Shutterstock.com/ID/BR

The fox is known to be **cunning**.

D

dancer (n) dançarino(a)
Day of the Dead (n) Dia de Finados
death (n) morte
dentist (n) dentista
dependable (adj) de confiança

Anyaivanova/Shutterstock.com/ID/BR

Scientists only use **dependable** data for their researches.

dining room (n) sala de jantar
director (n) diretor(a)
disrespectful (adj) desrespeitoso(a)
do the cooking (v) cozinhar
do the dishes (v) lavar a louça
documentary (n) documentário

Fac-símile/ID/BR

Ladies first is a **documentary** about a woman archer from India.

drums (n) tambores, bateria
dust the furniture (v) tirar o pó dos móveis

E

ear (n) orelha, ouvido
earache (n) dor de ouvido
Easter (n) Páscoa
Easter bunny (n) coelhinho da Páscoa
easy (adj) fácil
eat (v) comer
editor (n) editor(a)
elbow (n) cotovelo
engineer (n) engenheiro(a)
ENT (ear-nose-throat) doctor (n) otorrinolaringologista
enthusiastic (adj) entusiasmado(a)
environment (n) meio ambiente
exciting (adj) emocionante, excitante
expensive (adj) caro(a)
eye (n) olho
eye doctor (n) oftalmologista
eyebrow (n) sobrancelha
eyelash (n) cílio
eyelid (n) pálpebra

F

face (n) rosto
fall (n) outono
famous (adj) famoso(a)
fast (adj) rápido(a)
fat (adj) gordo(a)
Father's Day (n) Dia dos Pais
feet (n) pés
ferryboat/ferry (n) balsa

Tynka/Shutterstock.com/ID/BR

I went to the island on a **ferry**.

film (n) filme
finger (n) dedo
firefighter (n) bombeiro(a)
fireworks (n) fogos de artifício
fish (n) peixe
flag (n) bandeira
Flag Day (n) Dia da Bandeira
foot (n) pé
football player (n) jogador(a) de futebol
forehead (n) testa
friendly (adj) amigável, simpático(a)

Pixelheadphoto digitalskillet/Shutterstock.com/ID/BR

Everyone likes my father because he is nice and **friendly**.

fruit (n) fruta
funny (adj) engraçado(a)

G

garage (n) garagem
garden (n) jardim
get up (phr v) levantar-se
ghost (n) fantasma
gift (n) presente
go (v) ir
go out (phr v) sair (para passear)
good (adj) bom, boa
grain (n) grão

H

hair (n) cabelo
hall (n) salão, saguão
hand (n) mão
hang on (phr v) esperar
hang up (phr v) encerrar a ligação telefônica
hard (adj) duro(a), difícil
hate (v) detestar
have (v) ter
head (n) cabeça
headache (n) dor de cabeça
health (n) saúde
healthy (adj) saudável

Alex Brylov/Shutterstock.com/ID/BR

Meg loves to climb. She's very **healthy**.

heart (n) coração
heartache (n) desgosto, mágoa
heel (n) calcanhar
help (v) ajudar
hip (n) quadril
horse (n) cavalo
hunger (n) fome

I

ice cream (n) sorvete
Independence Day (n) Dia da Independência
interested (adj) interessado(a)
IT specialist (n) especialista em TI (tecnologia da informação)

J

jaw (n) mandíbula

K

keep down (phr v) manter em volume baixo

kidney (n) rim
kitchen (n) cozinha
knee (n) joelho
knife (n) faca

L

Labor Day (n) Dia do Trabalho
large (adj) grande
late (adj) atrasado(a)
late (adv) tarde
laundry room (n) lavanderia
lazy (adj) preguiçoso(a)
leg (n) perna
library (n) biblioteca
like (v) gostar
lips (n) lábios
listen (v) escutar, ouvir
liver (n) fígado
living room (n) sala de estar
log on (phr v) conectar-se a um *site*
look (v) olhar
love (v) amar, gostar muito
lovely (adj) adorável
lung (n) pulmão

M

make the bed (v) arrumar a cama
make-up artist (n) maquiador(a)
manual labor (n) trabalho manual
mask (n) máscara
massage therapist (n) massagista
meal (n) refeição

Francesco83/Shutterstock.com/ID/BR

I love to prepare a fresh **meal** for myself every day.

meat (n) carne
mechanic (n) mecânico(a)
milk (n) leite
model (n) modelo
mop the floor (v) limpar o chão

Andrey_Popov/Shutterstock.com/ID/BR

I **mopped the floor** to remove the dirt.

Mother's Day (n) Dia das Mães
motorcycle (n) motocicleta
mountain (n) montanha
mouth (n) boca
movie star (n) estrela de cinema
music program (n) musical de TV
musician (n) músico(a)

N

narrow-minded (adj) bitolado(a), limitado(a)
neck (n) pescoço
neighbor (n) vizinho(a)
New Year's Day (n) Dia de Ano-Novo
nickname (n) apelido
nose (n) nariz
nurse (n) enfermeiro(a)

O

oils (n) óleos, gorduras
old (adj) velho(a)
open-minded (adj) liberal, imparcial
orthopedist (n) ortopedista
overweight (adj) acima do peso

P

package (n) embalagem
painter (n) pintor(a)
parade (n) desfile
parents (n) pais
park (n) parque
pasta (n) massa, macarrão
photographer (n) fotógrafo(a)
physician (n) clínico geral
physiotherapist (n) fisioterapeuta
pick up the toys (v) pegar os brinquedos
plane (n) avião
plastic surgeon (n) cirurgião/cirurgiã plástico(a)
play (v) brincar, jogar, tocar (um instrumento musical)
polish the furniture (v) lustrar os móveis
producer (n) produtor(a)
pull the weeds (v) arrancar o mato

Liudmila Pereginskaya/Shutterstock.com/ID/BR

Gloria **pulls the weeds** every Sunday.

pumpkin pie (n) torta de abóbora

Q

quiz show (n) programa de perguntas e respostas

R

rake the leaves (v) juntar as folhas com o ancinho
read (v) ler
referee (n) juiz/juíza de futebol

Natursports/Shutterstock.com/ID/BR

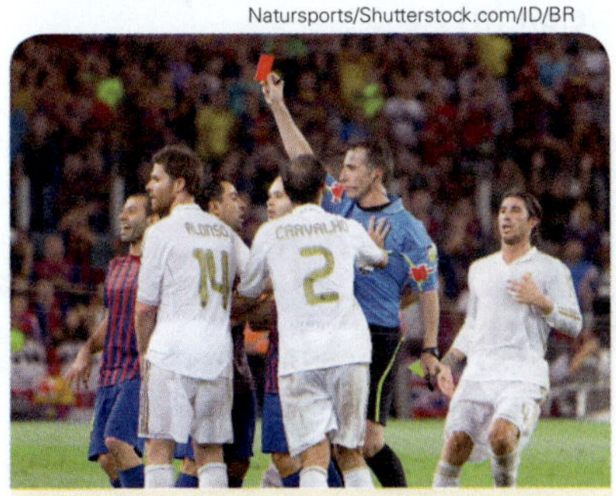

The **referee** is responsible for give the red card for a player.

reindeer (n) rena
relatives (n) parentes
respectful (adj) respeitoso(a)
rights (n) direitos

S

Santa Claus (n) Papai Noel
scary (adj) assustador(a)

science fiction/sci-fi (n) ficção científica
scientist (n) cientista
scroll down (phr v) correr a tela para baixo
see (v) ver
selfish (adj) egoísta
selfless (adj) generoso(a), altruísta
senior citizen (n) idoso(a)
series (n) seriado de TV
set the table (v) arrumar a mesa

Cultura Motion/Shutterstock.com/ID/BR

Set the table is a task that young teens can do.

set to (phr v) programar
ship (n) navio
shoulder (n) ombro
silly (adj) tolo(a)
singer (n) cantor(a)
sitcom (n) seriado cômico (comédia de situação)
skip (v) pular
sleigh (n) trenó

Vectorfusionart/Shutterstock.com/ID/BR

Santa Claus uses a **sleigh** to deliver all the presents.

soap opera (n) novela
sore throat (n) dor de garganta
speak up (phr v) falar mais alto
sports program (n) programa esportivo de TV
spring (n) primavera
square dance (n) quadrilha (dança típica)
stairs (n) escadas
stocking (n) meia
stomach (n) estômago
stomachache (n) dor de estômago
stretch (v) alongar
study (v) estudar
submarine (n) submarino
successful (adj) bem-sucedido(a)
sugar (n) açúcar
summer (n) verão
sweep the floor (v) varrer o chão
swim (v) nadar
switch off (phr v) desligar
switch on (phr v) ligar

T

take out the garbage (v) tirar o lixo
talented (adj) talentoso(a)
talk show (n) programa de entrevistas
tall (adj) alto(a)
tambourine (n) pandeiro
taxi driver (n) motorista de táxi
teacher (n) professor(a)
teeth (n) dentes
telemarketing operator (n) operador(a) de telemarketing

ESB Professional/Shutterstock.com/ID/BR

Giant companies always hire many **telemarketing operators**.

the news (n) noticiário
thigh (n) coxa
thin (adj) magro(a)
thriller (n) suspense
thumb (n) polegar
toe (n) dedo do pé
tooth (n) dente
toothache (n) dor de dente
train (n) trem
travel (v) viajar
truck (n) caminhão
turkey (n) peru
turn down (phr v) abaixar (o volume)
turn off (phr v) desligar
turn on (phr v) ligar
turn up (phr v) aumentar (o volume)
TV host (n) apresentador(a) de TV

U

ugly (adj) feio(a)
uncooperative (adj) não cooperativo(a)
undependable (adj) não confiável
understanding (adj) compreensivo(a)
unenthusiastic (adj) desanimado(a)
unfriendly (adj) antipático(a)

V

vacation (n) férias
vacuum the carpet (v) passar o aspirador no tapete
Valentine's Day (n) Dia dos Namorados (e dos amigos, nos Estados Unidos)
vendor (n) vendedor(a)
vegetable (n) legume
violent (adj) violento(a)
visit (v) visitar
volunteer work (n) trabalho voluntário

W

walk (v) andar
war (n) guerra
wash the clothes (v) lavar as roupas
watch (v) assistir
water (n) água
waterfall (n) cachoeira
weather (n) tempo (meteorológico)
well-trained (adj) bem treinado(a)
western (n) filme de faroeste
wildlife (n) vida selvagem
winter (n) inverno
wipe the walls (v) limpar as paredes
witch (n) bruxa
wrist (n) pulso
writer (n) escritor(a)

Y

yacht (n) iate
yoghurt (n) iogurte

Z

zoo (n) zoológico

Ideas for reading

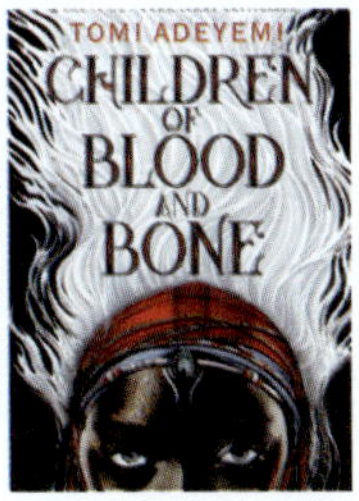

Editora Molino/Arquivo da editora

▸ Adeyemi, Tomi. *Children of Blood and Bone*. New York: Henry Holt and Co., 2018.

Four children in a journey full of violence, betrayal, and friendship. Enriched with themes presented in today's social and political landscape, the book takes on injustice, discrimination, and a struggle for change.

Editora Viking Books for Young Readers/Arquivo da editora

▸ Ahmadi, Arvin. *Down and Across*. Toronto: Viking Books for Young Readers, 2018.

Scott Ferdowsi, a man who usually gives up, moves on to Washington seeking guidance from a famous psychologist who claims to know the secret to success. He meets Fiora, a college student that will make him think and live differently.

Editora Flatiron Books/Arquivo da editora

▸ Albert, Melissa. *The Hazel Wood*: a Novel. New York: Flatiron Books, 2018.

When Alice's grandmother dies alone on her estate, Alice learns how bad her luck can really get: her mother is stolen away by a figure who claims to come from the cruel supernatural world where her grandmother's stories are set.

Editora Walden Pond Press/Arquivo da editora

▸ Anderson, John David. *Sidekicked*. New York: Walden Pond Press, 2014.

Andrew Bean is a teenager who is part of a secret organization for the training of superhero sidekicks. His power is the possession of super senses. Even so, he has to deal with all the high school's problems.

Editora Little Brown and Company/Arquivo da editora

▸ Bacigalupi, Paolo. *Ship Breaker*. New York: Little, Brown Books for Young Readers, 2011.

Nailer one day discovers an exquisite clipper ship beached during a recent hurricane. He faces a very important decision: strip the ship for all it's worth or rescue its lone survivor, a wealthy girl who could lead him to a better life.

Editora Nancy Paulsen Books/Arquivo da editora

▸ Grimes, Nikki. *Between the Lines*. New York: Nancy Paulsen Books, 2018.

Darrian dreams of writing for *The New York Times*. To hone his skills and learn more about the power of words, he enrolls in a class where every student has something important to say. Sharing their poetry, they learn that they all face challenges and have a story to tell.

Editora Dial Books/Arquivo da editora

▸ Hiranandani, Veera. *The Night Diary*. New York: Dial Books, 2018.

Nisha, a twelve-year-old half-Muslim, half-Hindu, and her family leave the country they lived, because of wars. In a long, difficult and dangerous journey, Nisha still believes in good things.

Editora Scholastic Press/Arquivo da editora

▸ Korman, Gordon. *Restart*. New York: Scholastic Press, 2018.

One day, Chase wakes up in a hospital room and he doesn't remember anything, not even who he is. He has to learn his own life again. When he backs to school, many things are different... People look at him in a different way. But why? What did happen that day?

Editora Feiwel & Friendss/Arquivo da editora

▸ Meyer, Marissa. *Renegades*. New York: Feiwel & Friends, 2017.

The Renegades are a syndicate of humans with extraordinary abilities who emerged from the ruins of a crumbled society. As champions of justice, they remain a symbol of hope and courage to everyone... except the villains they once overthrew.

Editora Text Publishing/Arquivo da editora

▸ Saeed, Aisha. *Amal Unbound*. London: Nancy Paulsen Books, 2018.

Amal's dream is to become a teacher. Her dreams are temporarily dashed when she must stay home from school to take care of her siblings. Amal is upset, but she doesn't lose hope and finds ways to continue learning.

Não escreva no livro.

Dictionaries

- *Dicionário Collins inglês-português/português-inglês.* São Paulo: Disal, 2012.

- *Dicionário Longman escolar inglês-português/português-inglês.* São Paulo: Longman, 2008.

- *Dicionário Oxford escolar para estudantes brasileiros de inglês* – Português-Inglês/ Inglês-Português. Oxford: Oxford University Press, 2009.

- *Dicionário Scottini escolar de inglês.* Blumenau: Todolivro, 2017.

- Kernerman, L. *Password*: English Dictionary for Speakers of Portuguese. São Paulo: Martins Fontes, 2010.

- Marques, A. *Dicionário de inglês-português/português-inglês.* São Paulo: Ática, 2005.

Online dictionaries

- *Cambridge Dictionaries Online.* Disponível em: https://dictionary.cambridge.org. Oferece dicionários monolíngue (inglês-inglês) e bilíngue (inglês-português).

- *Internet Picture Dictionary.* Disponível em: http://pdictionary.com. Dicionário ilustrado monolíngue (inglês-inglês).

- *Linguee.* Disponível em: https://www.linguee.com.br/portugues-ingles. Ferramenta de tradução inglês-português e português-inglês (por meio de buscador).

- *Merriam-Webster.* Disponível em: https://www.merriam-webster.com. Dicionário monolíngue (inglês-inglês) com etimologia e frequência de uso das palavras.

- *Michaelis Moderno Dicionário Inglês.* Disponível em: https://michaelis.uol.com.br/moderno-ingles/. Dicionário bilíngue (inglês-português/português-inglês).

- *Oxford Living Dictionaries – English.* Disponível em: https://www.lexico.com. Apresenta dicionário monolíngue (inglês-inglês).

- *Word Reference.* Disponível em: https://www.wordreference.com. Dicionário multilíngue (inglês-diversas línguas) com diferentes acepções e usos.

Acessos em: 3 mar. 2022.

Useful links

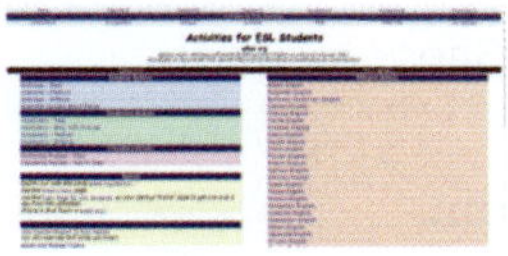

Arquivo/A4esl

Activities for ESL Students. http://a4esl.org

Traz mais de mil testes, exercícios e quebra-cabeças de gramática e vocabulário para a prática do inglês.

Arquivo/Eslcafe

Dave's ESL Cafe. https://www.eslcafe.com

O *site* traz uma seção exclusiva para o estudante, com conteúdos que incluem expressões idiomáticas, *phrasal verbs*, pronúncia, gírias, fóruns e vários tipos de *quiz*. Explore-a!

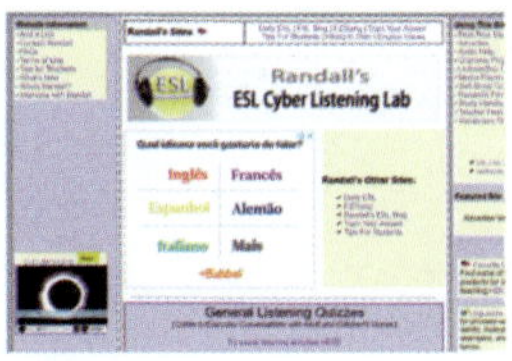

Arquivo/Esl-lab

ESL Cyber Listening Lab. https://www.esl-lab.com

É um bom recurso para quem quer praticar a compreensão oral (*listening*). O *site* pode ser considerado um laboratório virtual.

Arquivo/Short-Stories

Short Stories. http://www.eastoftheweb.com/short-stories/

Traz narrações curtas de vários gêneros literários, atividades de compreensão e jogos em inglês.

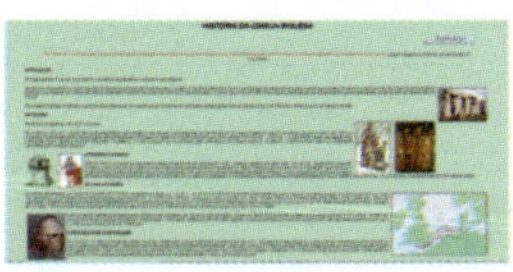

Arquivo/Sk

História da Língua Inglesa. https://www.sk.com.br/sk-historia-da-lingua-inglesa.html

O conteúdo dessa seção é altamente relevante, com texto em português. Fala da história da língua inglesa desde os celtas até os dias de hoje e traz várias ilustrações. Descubra um pouco mais da história da língua que estamos estudando!

Arquivo/Learnenglish

LearnEnglish. https://learnenglish.britishcouncil.org

Traz conteúdo bem variado para aprendizado e prática de inglês. Por exemplo, *Listen & Watch*, *Grammar & Vocabulary*, *Fun & Games*. Vale a pena conferir.

Arquivo/Kids.nationalgeographic

National Geographic Kids https://kids.nationalgeographic.com

Esse *site* é visualmente muito bonito e vale a pena explorar seu conteúdo, que possibilita aprender sobre países, animais e outros assuntos.

Arquivo/Eflnet

Picture Vocabulary. https://eflnet.com/vocabulary

É um *picture dictionary* organizado por categorias. Ao clicar em uma gravura, um arquivo de voz reproduz a pronúncia da palavra.

Arquivo/Planetpals

Planet Pals.com. http://www.planetpals.com/planet.html

Contém muitas informações sobre o meio ambiente, apresentadas com uma linguagem própria para o público pré-adolescente.

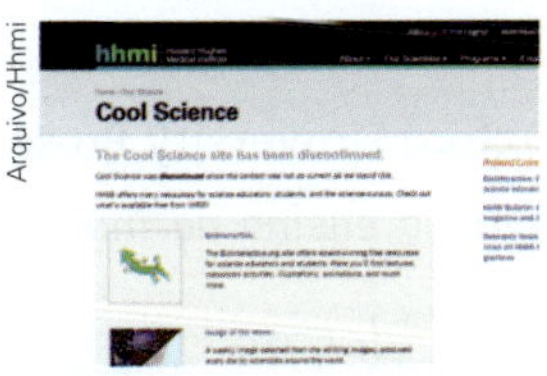

Arquivo/Hhmi

Science for Kids. https://www.sciencekids.co.nz

Se você se interessa por ciências, com certeza vai gostar de fazer as experiências, *quizzes*, jogos e projetos propostos nesse *site*. Além disso, há uma seção chamada *Fun Stuff*! para você se divertir com o tema.

Acessos em: 3 mar. 2022.

Bibliography

ABSY, C. A. *et al. Leitura em língua inglesa*: uma abordagem instrumental. São Paulo: Disal, 2010.

ANTUNES, I. *Muito além da gramática*: por um ensino de línguas sem pedras no caminho. São Paulo: Parábola Editorial, 2007. (Série Estratégias de Ensino.)

ARNOLD, J.; PUCHTA, H.; RINVOLUCRI, M. *Imagine that!*: mental imagery in the EFL classroom. Cambridge: Cambridge University Press, 2007.

BEZERRA, M. A.; DIONISIO, A. P.; MACHADO, A. R. (org.). *Gêneros textuais & ensino*. São Paulo: Parábola Editorial, 2010.

BRASIL. Secretaria de Educação Básica. *Base Nacional Comum Curricular*: educação é a base. Brasília: MEC, 2022. Disponível em: http://basenacionalcomum.mec.gov.br/images/BNCC_EI_EF_110518_versaofinal_site.pdf. Acesso em: 5 abr. 2022.

CAMPBELL, C.; KRYSZEWSKA, H. *Learner-based teaching*. Oxford: Oxford University Press, 2003.

CELANI, M. A. A. *Reflexões e ações (trans)formadoras no ensino-aprendizagem de inglês*. Campinas: Mercado de Letras, 2010

CROSS, D. *Large classes in action*. Hertfordshire: Prentice Hall International, 1995.

DUFF, A.; MALEY, A. *Literature*. Oxford: Oxford University Press, 1990.

GONTOW, C. *The classroom is a stage*: 40 short plays for English students. São Paulo: Disal, 2019.

GRELLET, F. *Developing reading skills*. Cambridge: Cambridge University Press, 1981.

GRIFFEE, D. T. *Songs in action*. Hertfordshire: Prentice Hall International, 1992.

HARMER, J. *How to teach English*. London: Pearson Education, 2007.

HOLDEN, S. *O ensino da língua inglesa nos dias atuais*. São Paulo: SBS, 2009.

HOLDER, V. *Grammar on the go*: quick and easy blackboard activities. New York: Addison--Wesley, 1995.

KEDDIE, J. *Images*. Oxford: Oxford University Press, 2009.

LAGO, A. *Jogos divertidos com material para sua aula de inglês*. São Paulo: Disal, 2019.

LAPKOSKI, G. A. O. *Do texto ao sentido*: teoria e prática de leitura em língua inglesa. Curitiba: Ibpex, 2011.

LIMA, D. C. *Inglês em escolas públicas não funciona?*: uma questão, múltiplos olhares. São Paulo: Parábola Editorial, 2011.

MARTINEZ, P. *Didática de línguas estrangeiras*. São Paulo: Parábola Editorial, 2009.

MATOS, F. G. *Criatividade no ensino de inglês*. São Paulo: Disal, 2019.

NAPOLITANO, M. *Como usar o cinema na sala de aula*. São Paulo: Contexto, 2005.

PAINTER, L. *Homework*. Oxford: Oxford University Press, 2003.

PRESCHER, E. *Jogos e atividades para o ensino de inglês*: 300 maneiras de estimular os seus alunos. São Paulo: Disal, 2019.

RICHARDS, J. C.; RENANDYA, W. A. (ed.). *Methodology in language teaching*: an anthology of current practice. New York: Cambridge University Press, 2002.

RODRIGUES, D. (org.). *Inclusão e educação*: doze olhares sobre a educação inclusiva. São Paulo: Summus, 2006.

SANTOS, D. *Como ler melhor em inglês*. São Paulo: Disal, 2019.

THIEL, G. C.; THIEL, J. C. *Movie takes*: a magia do cinema na sala de aula. Curitiba: Aymará, 2009.

TOMLINSON, B.; MASUHARA, H. *A elaboração de materiais para cursos de idiomas*. São Paulo: SBS, 2005.

WALESKO, A. M. H. *Compreensão oral em língua inglesa*. Curitiba: Ibpex, 2012.

WRIGHT, A. *Pictures for language learning*. Glasgow: Cambridge University Press, 1989.